Corinth Excavations
Archaeological Manual

CORINTH EXCAVATIONS
ARCHAEOLOGICAL MANUAL

Guy D.R. Sanders
Sarah A. James
Alicia Carter Johnson

With contributions by
Ioulia Tzonou-Herbst
James Herbst
Nicol Anastasatou
Katerina Ragkou

The Digital Press at the University of North Dakota
Grand Forks, ND

2017 The Digital Press @ The University of North Dakota

ISBN-13:978-0692878101 (Digital Press at The University of North Dakota, The)

ISBN-10:0692878106

Library of Congress Control Number: 2017906025
Digital Press at The University of North Dakota, The,
Grand Forks, ND

CONTENTS

About This Book

This book is the faithful reproduction of the Corinth Excavation's Archaeological Manual. As such, it is designed to be used on a very specific project with a particular organization and goals. References to specific forms, called "sheets" used on the project appear in small caps (e.g. CUT SHEET) and are reproduced both in the Appendix and as a separate download (accessible at https://perma.cc/35EF-LREC or the QR code below). Individual fields on those sheets are also in all small caps (e.g. NOTES). The numbers on the forms coincide with the reference numbers of each section of the Archaeological Manual.

Our hope in publishing this manual is to make this manual available for citation, to capture a moment in time in the history and methods of Corinth Excavations, and to encourage other archaeological projects to publish their field manuals.

Preface

This manual describes the present state of archaeological practice at ancient Corinth, Greece. The system employed here has evolved over five decades of excavation and in response to both the nature of the anthropogenic activities and the ultimate goals of the excavation: a diachronic archaeological and cultural history of Corinth. The practicalities of removing archaeological material from the ground, recording it, analyzing it, and storing it for future use have been developed over the past 100-plus years of archaeological exploration, and they are well-suited to the field here, to the post-excavation methods used, and to the facilities available at Corinth. Previous field and recording strategies owe a debt to the Gezer system (Dever and Lance 1978). The current field methods employed are influenced by the strategies and processes advocated by Philip Barker (1997) and Edward Harris (1989), among others. Our current recording system has been developed to best facilitate single-context recording and to enable excavation data to be searchable in database format. Aspects of the field recording system have been adapted for use at Corinth from the archaeological site manual of the Museum of London Archaeology Service (MOLAS) (Spence 1994). Modifications to the open-area strategy and the MOLAS recording system are the product of accumulated experience of excavations in Greece, the United States, Britain, the Near East, and Cyprus as well as in response to the specific conditions that exist at Corinth Excavations and impact archaeological research here. This manual is intended to be of particular use to archaeologists working in Greece and the Mediterranean region and addresses issues of site formation particular to this part of the world. Corinth Excavations would like to acknowledge the work of A. Rohn, and E. Barnes for their contributions toward our current recording system for burials and human remains.

G.D.R. Sanders
S. A. James
A. Carter Johnson
I. Tzonou-Herbst
J. Herbst
N. Anastasatou

1. METHODOLOGY

1.1. STRATIGRAPHIC EXCAVATION

Archaeological sites are made up of discrete layers of cultural debris and other natural features, such as deposits formed by erosion. Stratigraphic excavation is the isolation and identification of different deposits and features and the careful removal of each of these separately in the reverse order of their deposition, the logical assumption being that the upper strata were formed more recently than the lower strata. This concept was developed for application in archaeology from the Law of Superposition, a geological concept relating to the formation of horizontal layers of rock in the earth's crust. In plain language, the "Last In, First Out" principle means that a pit must be isolated and dug before the earth into which it was cut is excavated. This is the basic tenet of modern archaeological excavation.

1.2. THE OPEN–AREA METHOD

Traditionally, archaeologists in Greece have used trenches and balks to excavate ancient remains (i.e. the trench-and-balk method). These typically take the form of 5-x-5-m squares with balks that separate them (Fig. 1a), and they are commonly referred to also as "Wheeler boxes," in reference to Sir Mortimer Wheeler, the British archaeologist who first pioneered their use in the 1920s and 1930s (Wheeler 1954). Proponents of this method argue that the balks allow the archaeologist to have permanent access to the stratigraphy of the site by preserving vertical views of the strata throughout excavation. While sections can be a useful tool, they also may be a hindrance to the archaeologist.

With this method, ironically, the archaeological remains that have not been excavated (i.e. the balks) can be given more importance by the archaeologist than what has actually been excavated (i.e. the trenches). However, it has been demonstrated repeatedly that the vertical section preserved by the balk can be more misleading in terms of understanding site formation than can simply excavating context by context without creating arbitrary trench boundaries. The reasons for this include situations when the balk "just misses" a context that was excavated inside the trench, and therefore the section preserves a false or incomplete record of the stratigraphic relationships of the contexts in that area. The trench-and-balk method also may impede the interpretation of certain contexts, wherein only part of the context is revealed inside the trench.

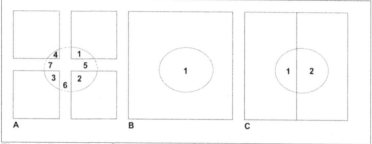

Figure 1. Excavation of a pit using (a) the trench-and-balk method (8 contexts), (b) the open-area method (1 context), and (c) the modified trench-and-balk method (2 contexts). Drawing J. Herbst

At Corinth, we have recently reassessed our own methodology and abandoned the trench-and-balk method in favor of the open-area method (Fig. 1b), now standard practice all over Britain, much of the United States, and other parts of Europe. Instead of arbitrarily sectioning all the stratigraphic contexts on the site and removing them within a single trench, open-area excavation treats the entire excavation area as one large trench, in which each individual context is identified, recorded, and removed (if possible) in chronological and stratigraphic sequence. This method allows us to see more, if not all, of a given context at one time, and it thus provides more information at the moment of excavation that can be used to interpret context formation, finds, and stratigraphic relationships. It also allows for a better chronological control of the site; that is, it is possible to concentrate attention on the stratigraphic relationships and material record of a single chronological period, rather than excavating several trenches at different chronological levels and leaving the excavators to piece the disparate records back together after the excavation season has ended.

However, it is important for the method to be flexible enough to manage the variety of situations that will be encountered in the field. There may be specific situations in which it is helpful to section a context or a series of contexts in order to obtain a vertical view of the strata before the entirety of the material is removed (Fig. 1c). This strategy might be useful when an area of the site has a particularly complicated stratigraphy, when a section might be useful for soil coring, or when the importance of a feature must be evaluated in a time-limited excavation. If this strategy is employed, it is important that the decision is fully explained on the context recording sheets (see §1.3) and that the scarp created through such excavation is carefully drawn. Later on, it also will be important to reunite the material taken from the sectioned contexts, be they in two or four parts (i.e. by half-sectioning or quarter-sectioning).

At the densely inhabited, architecturally rich urban site of Corinth, we have come to recognize open-area excavation as the most appropriate excavation strategy, as it allows for more successful on-site and post-excavation interpretation and analysis and reduces the time needed to publish findings. The open-area strategy might not produce the results desired on other archaeological research projects, where constraints on time and resources and a lack of experienced excavators may impede the implementation of this practice. However, the procedures outlined in this manual are not exclusive to open-area excavation, as the rigorous recording methodology advocated here makes comparison of strata between excavated areas more straightforward on any given excavated site.

1.3. SINGLE-CONTEXT RECORDING

Any action that leaves a trace in the strata of an archae-ological site, whether it be an anthropogenic or natural event, should be recorded during excavation; in this system, such an action is called a **context**. Some actions will leave a "positive" trace: these are either **deposits** of soil and other materials, such as a dump of rubbish in a pit or the fill inside a grave, or built **structures**, such as walls. Others actions will leave a "negative" trace: these are cuts, or an action that "cuts" into other contexts (i.e. when a grave, well, or foundation trench for the building of a wall is dug into the surrounding contexts). By identifying, excavating, and recording each context individually, it is possible to reconstruct the history of activity at a site. Each context is recorded on one of three standardized context recording sheets (the DEPOSIT SHEET, CUT SHEET, OR STRUCTURE SHEET; see Appendix 1), which encourages the recorder to make certain observations and attempt certain interpretations. Each context is also drawn to scale. In theory, by keeping consistent, careful, and detailed records, it should be possible at any time in the future to reconstruct the site layer by layer and context by context, integrating finds and features. In an open-area excavation, deposits are recorded and removed in their entirety. However, in practice, certain walls and features may be left for future restoration and presentation to the public, making total removal of these contexts impossible.

Experienced archaeological technicians trained by Corinth Excavations and overseen by the foreman do the exca-vating at Corinth. However, supervisors also do a certain amount of excavation. Although their main responsibility is to record individual contexts as they are removed, exca-vation will help them to understand differences in color, composition, and texture that differentiate deposits and define cuts. The Director of Excavations and the Field Director are responsible for assessing the stratigraphic relationships of the excavation area as a whole and for coordinating the supervisors in the recording of contexts as they are removed in stratigraphic sequence. The Corinth Excavations recording system aims to counter the potential problem of a disconnect between an experienced excavator and an inexperienced recorder by forcing the recorder to answer specific questions about every context—questions that are impossible to answer without the recorder feeling the soil themselves, working very closely with the excavator to understand the physical nature of the context and how it relates to surrounding contexts, and suggesting the most plausible interpretation of the context based on all available evidence.

1.4. THE HARRIS MATRIX

In 1975 Edward Harris published and copyrighted the Harris-Winchester Matrix (Harris 1975). At Corinth, the Harris Matrix is one of the principal post-excavation analytical processes, and it is something that must be added to and updated in and out of the field on a daily basis. The Harris Matrix is not a matrix at all, but rather a two-dimensional diagram that represents the spatial and temporal relationships between archaeological contexts. This is why in every Harris Matrix the latest contexts should be at the top and the earlier ones below (see diagram below). Since 1975 numerous books and articles have been written on the subject, and several computer programs have been designed to help assemble the diagrams. The Corinth Excavations database tracks stratigraphic relationships (see §6.2.10). Because the database does not yet generate a Harris Matrix for graphic feedback, a master matrix must be created on paper or on the computer. At Corinth we regularly use a program called ArchEd (first developed in 1996 at the Max Planck Institute) to render Harris matrices graphically. All contexts are included in the matrix: deposits, cuts, and structures. Every one of these contexts should have a unique context number.

There are four basic time relationships that exist between contexts:

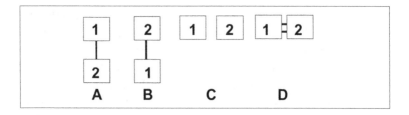

A. **1 is later than 2.** This is an immediate chronological relationship.
B. **1 is earlier than 2.** This is an immediate chronological relationship.
C. **1 is contemporary with 2.** This relationship can only be determined by material culture or a full understanding of the site (e.g. two walls bond with each other, and so must have been constructed at the same time).
D. **1 equals 2.** In other words, this is the same context excavated in two operations, such as when a context is sectioned or when the same context has been cut into two parts by later human activity (e.g. a construction trench for a drain that cuts through an earlier grave, rendering it in two parts).

When constructing a Harris Matrix, it is not necessarily the physical relationship that is the most important element. A context may overlie several strata, but it is the latest of these strata that is the most chronologically relevant. For example, if the foundation trench for a wall cuts through several different layers of soil, it is critical to establish **the latest layer that it cuts**—this was the surface that was in use at the time the wall was built, and therefore it is the most useful in dating the construction of the wall. In this way, the matrix is a very important organizational tool, as it moves beyond simple physical relationships and forces excavators to refine their understanding of chronological relationships. The Harris Matrix should be **updated daily** by the excavator to help maintain a working understanding of the stratigraphy of the site. WORKING HARRIS MATRIX SHEETS are available for use in the field as a supplement to the Harris Matrix component of the context recording sheets (Appendix 1).

Example: In the section illustrated below (Fig. 2), the topsoil (Context 1) is the latest context present. Context 1 overlies several discrete deposits (2, 3, 4, and 10), physically touching all of them. Through further excavation, it is revealed that 2 cuts 10 and thus must be later in time. Further, 2 and 3 both cut into 4, 4 overlies 5, 5 cuts 6 and 7, and so on. However, in the Harris Matrix for this hypothetical situation, the relationships have been streamlined so that redundant relationships are not expressed. In this case, even though it has already been established that 1 is later than 2, 3, 4, and 10, it is unnecessary to draw additional lines from 1 to 4 and from 1 to 10, as the matrix is already expressing the fact that 1 is later in time than both 4 and

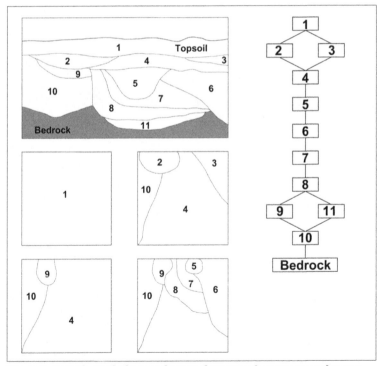

Figure 2. Hypothetical plans and vertical section showing several strata overlying bedrock, with a Harris Matrix expressing these relationships. Drawing J. Herbst

10 by being situated above them in the diagram. (Note that cuts are not included in this example.)

2. GENERAL EXCAVATION PROCEDURES

2.1. GENERAL GUIDELINES

Cleanliness is next to godliness on an archaeological site. A few millimeters of dust or loose soil on the surface of the excavated area can obscure soil changes completely and make stratigraphic excavation impossible. **Make sure to sweep often** (see §2.3 for instructions on recording archaeological cleaning). It is also very dangerous to allow loose soil to accumulate around the edge of the excavation. This will happen naturally as foot traffic disturbs dry soil, but it is very important for the edges of the excavation to be swept back regularly to prevent topsoil material from falling into the freshly excavated areas, and thereby contaminating the contexts revealed below.

The hot and dry climate of Greece and the Mediterranean region as a whole makes it difficult to see the stratigraphy of the site—and especially color changes—as dry soil loses much of the color is has when moist. **The soil should be sprayed with water when this becomes a problem.**

Ideally, it will be possible to recognize each archaeological context on site by its unique physical properties (i.e. appearance or texture) and to remove it neatly. In practice, however, some stratigraphic relationships will be difficult to discern without careful exploration of the boundaries with other contexts. In situations where it is difficult to find the edges between similar contexts, the junctions should be explored carefully until the boundaries can be established with certainty.

There may be times, however, when an error will have been made in deciding which context is stratigraphically the latest. When an error is recognized, excavation of the context should be stopped immediately and no more material collected. The error must be described in the NOTES field on the context recording sheets: specifically, when and how the error was identified and the course of action needed to rectify the mistake. A new context number with new measurements must be registered in order to continue excavation, and changes must be made as appropriate to the new understanding of the stratigraphic sequence. Be sure that the Harris Matrix reflects the new understanding of the stratigraphic sequence, and not simply the order of excavation (which in some cases may be erroneous).

Since contexts are dated by the latest material contained within them, it is essential to avoid **contamination** in the form of later and stratigraphically different material (particularly pottery) mistakenly collected with any given context. Make sure, therefore, that **all** the soil from a specific context is removed before the context is closed and excavation continues with a new context.

As the removal of different contexts on site is recorded, keep in mind that what is written in the field will be examined, analyzed, and weighed by future scholars wishing to publish the archaeological material of Corinth and understand aspects of the development of the site. A future researcher may be interested in a specific context and the materials contained within it, as well as the context's relation to other deposits and features. For example, a future scholar interested in dating a wall will want to know if a certain context is a floor, and (1) if the floor is cut by a foundation trench for a wall, (2) if the floor goes directly up to the wall or over the cut of the foundation trench, or (3) if the floor goes over the top of the wall. In example (1), the floor pre-dates the wall. Any context that is cut by the foundation trench must have existed before the wall was built, and finds from these contexts could give a "pre-occupation" date (the terminus post quem for the structure). In example (2), the floor was laid after the foundation trench was dug and the wall was built, and all three are part of the same structure. Any finds from this floor are from the use phase of the building. In example (3), the floor is covering the top of a wall that is part of an earlier building. Finds from above the floor will help date the abandonment of the structure (i.e. its terminus ante quem). Describing the relationships between contexts during excavation therefore requires interpreting not only the function and formation of the context being recorded, but also its role in the greater web of human activity in this area over time.

On the DEPOSIT SHEET, the recorder's interpretations should be stated and evidence given in support of them, but sometimes it is only possible to fully interpret a context after it is excavated, its pottery and finds are analyzed, and related contexts are similarly studied. When this is the case, it is crucial that the new interpretation be added to the NOTES field on the same DEPOSIT SHEET and context record in the database. These additions must be labeled "Later Notes" so that is clear to anyone consulting the records in the future which comments were an interpretation made in the field and which were added later. Be sure to initial and date all "Later Notes."

During the recording process, both in the field and out, it is important to communicate with fellow excavators, recorders, and supervisors as, ultimately, all contexts that are excavated contemporaneously are related in some manner, and these relationships are crucial to understanding the site as a whole.

2.2. COORDINATE GRID MEASUREMENTS AND ELEVATIONS

Every context should have a plan. At Corinth, all plan measurements are related to a Cartesian coordinate grid system. Each point measurement is determined uniquely in a plane through two numbers: an X-axis value (easting) and a Y-axis value (northing). Thus, for example, a point in the excavation could be designated as: E265.76, N1003.57. The grid used at Corinth is also a reference to the grid on the

Hellenic Military Geographical Services 1:50,000 Korinthia map, which is in the HATT projection but is easily converted to the newer ΕΓΣΑ87 projection. Because the values in the system are large and unwieldy (e.g. E7043.76, N16362.75), a benchmark closer to the grid for the ancient site has been established to keep the numbers small and with positive values. For the sake of uniformity with other work on the site since 1960, all elevation measurements are related to the benchmarks established by the Hellenic Military Geographical Service monuments (Robinson and Weinberg 1960:238). Measurements are taken using a total station, and all context recording sheets and drawings reflect these benchmarks (eastings and northings are recorded in meters, and elevation in meters above sea level). **Measurements should always be taken to the nearest 0.01 m.**

All supervisors should learn how to use the total station at the beginning of the excavation season, as well as how to physically set up the machine and tripod and how to use the machine to take accurate readings using the reflective prism.

When a new context is excavated or described, **representative elevations must be taken** on the surface of the context; if the context runs into the edge of excavation, elevations must also be taken along that edge. Several representative bottom elevations must also be taken on the surface revealed by the removal of the context. In the case of a wall, elevations should be taken on the highest preserved stone, the last stone at both ends of the wall, and/or the last stone before the wall runs into the edge of excavation. While the STRUCTURE SHEET requires only maximum elevations and coordinates north and east of the permanent benchmark, several elevations should be taken on the surface of each context—as well as below it after it is removed—so that the general contours of each context can be reconstructed after excavation. These elevations must be recorded on the plan of each context using the appropriate drawing convention (see §6.2.3).

2.3. ARCHAEOLOGICAL CLEANING

There may be times when it is necessary to scrape or sweep down an area that is composed of several different soil contexts (e.g. to prepare a section for drawing or a large area of the site for photographing). Any material from this operation should be collected on its own and assigned a new unique context number; this will prevent it from being added to the material from another discrete context and thus contaminating it. If it is possible to ascertain **exactly** which contexts are contributing materials to this cleaning operation, these numbers should be entered in the NOTES field of the appropriate context recording sheet for the cleaning operation. While material collected during the cleaning of multiple contexts may not be useful for dating or interpreting an individual context on site, the material might be useful to the museum staff at the end of the season for the purposes of mending pottery or other finds, and so it is worth keeping at least temporarily.

Cleaning "contexts" are not included in the Harris Matrix because they are not true contexts, but rather units created as a means of tracking finds during cleaning. If the cleaning operation extends over multiple contexts, it is unnecessary to describe the soil in the relevant soil description fields on the various context sheets. However, measurements and elevations must still be entered on the DEPOSIT SHEET for each cleaning operation, and a description of the cleaning and why it was performed must be entered in the NOTES field.

2.4. BALKS

If the "Last In, First Out" principle cannot be followed for some reason, a protective strip of soil or a "skin balk" should be left around the later context while the earlier context is being excavated. Sometimes other techniques may also be employed to protect the archaeological integrity of the site, to prevent contamination, and to explore potentially important features within a reasonable time frame.

2.4.1. Skin Balks

Skin balks protect against contamination of the earlier context by creating a barrier between the earlier and later contexts. If the strip of soil is excavated later, it should be assigned its own context number and its relationship to the earlier and later contexts should be made clear in the NOTES and HARRIS MATRIX fields.

2.4.2. Pedestalling

In an ideal open-area excavation, pedestalling is unnecessary; however, in reality it is unavoidable in certain conditions. For example, it is against Greek law to remove a wall without a permit, and so at Corinth some walls must have skin balks and be pedestalled. Alternatively, an excavator may encounter an object (such as a large boulder) that cannot be removed safely for some reason; in this case, the object should be pedestalled and a skin balk used, if necessary.

2.4.3. Sectioning

In open-area excavation, sectioning is generally avoided because it is antithetical to the principle as a whole. However, it is occasionally a necessary and wise choice. At Corinth, contexts for which sectioning is appropriate include large pits and deep fills characteristic of the Late Roman and Medieval periods. In these cases, a section or sample of the pit or fill will often provide enough information to determine whether the entirety should be excavated. Before sectioning, the entire context should be drawn on a top plan and the area to be sectioned clearly indicated. Once completed, the section will reveal a scarp or vertical face (which can also occur when a skin balk is left in place). This vertical face (see §4.3) should be recorded with drawings and photographs.

2.5. DRY SIEVING

Dry sieving guarantees nearly complete retrieval of all archaeological material larger than the size of the sieve mesh from a given context. In addition to pottery and coins, dry sieving may recover other small objects that are impossible to recover manually, such as mammal and fish bones, glass, carbonized seeds, and eggshells. In addition, the recovery of carbonized finds and microfauna would indicate that water flotation (see §2.6) should be used on the context. Certain contexts will be more rewarding to sieve than others, and it is essential to consider the kind of data that is sought before determining the proportion, mesh size, and method of sieving. Primary deposits (**the fills of pits, hearths, floors, roads, foundation trenches, and the matrix of structures**) should be 100 percent dry sieved, with a portion sampled for water sieving. Secondary and disturbed deposits (**topsoil, agricultural plow zone, robbing trenches, dumped fill, and leveling fill**) should be sieved only when it is very important to establish a date for their deposition and to aid the understanding of the site's development. Secondary and disturbed deposits may contain an overwhelming amount of early material, and it may be important to see if there are any later pieces. In this case, a proportion can be sieved as an experiment, and if needed, 100 percent can be dry sieved. In other cases. sieving is a poor use of time and excavation resources. For example, sieving for pottery in a context composed of degraded mud brick will produce huge quantities of tiny sherds that were reused as temper and that predate the construction of the mud brick wall, but virtually no material useful in dating the context.

The reasons for sieving a particular context should be made explicit in the NOTES field on the DEPOSIT SHEET. In addition, the size of the mesh used (typically 5 mm) and the percentage of the total context that was sieved should be recorded in the DRY SIEVING field (see §6.2.14). The latter can be estimated by counting the number of buckets of soil removed.

2.6. WATER FLOTATION

A water flotation machine forces water upward from below a soil sample (Fig. 3). Light materials—such as small bones, seeds, and carbonized organic materials—float and are thus propelled by the flow of water toward collection sieves. The rest of the sample is washed clean of any soil, leaving behind heavier material—any larger microfauna, botanical material, and anthropogenic finds—that can be sorted once they are dry. Although limey soils, such as those at Corinth, are generally not good for pollen preservation, the microchemistry of certain contexts may be ideal. Regardless, the recovery of microfauna is an important part of understanding the archaeological record and the processes of site formation because it recovers artifacts and ecofacts not possible to obtain through dry sieving.

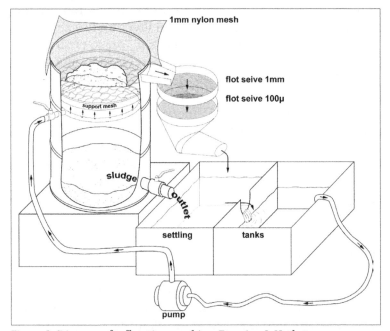

Figure 3. Diagram of a flotation machine. Drawing J. Herbst.

Certain deposits are better suited to water flotation than others. Deposits that should always be sampled include hearths, pits, sewers or drains, wells, floors and surfaces, depressions in floors, areas with a high concentration of burned material, storage and working areas, and the contents of whole vessels. If the fill of a pit or well is sampled, a sample of the context it cuts should also be taken for comparison. When a sample is taken for water flotation, all or a percentage of the remainder of the context must also be dry sieved. As a general rule, contexts should only be sampled if they are well stratified and constitute an archaeologically defined feature whose function and relationship to the site is understood. Sampling a random anomalous feature will not clarify its formation, and sampling a context that is poorly stratified will be of no help to the excavation. By keeping the Harris Matrix up-to-date, relationships between contexts will be transparent, thereby enabling the development of a more successful sampling strategy.

When taking a sample for water flotation, **the minimum sample size is 10 liters (about 2.5 gallons)**. The sample should be collected in plastic bags or buckets that are labeled with wooden tags. If the context is too small to remove 10 liters of earth, a percentage of the context may be sampled and this percentage noted in the PERCENT OF CONTEXT field on the SAMPLE SHEET. **One** SAMPLE SHEET **must be completed for each sample from a single context**.

In certain instances, such as a floor deposit or a kitchen, the water flotation sampling strategy may differ. The SAMPLE SHEET allows for such instances. In every context in which multiple water flotation samples are taken, a new sheet must be completed for each sample. In the special situations described above, such as a floor deposit, the location where the sample was taken from within the context should be indicated in the SKETCH PLAN field (see §2.6.1.11) on the SAMPLE SHEET.

Setting Up and Operating the Water Sieve for Flotation:
Instructions by Katerina Ragkou

The types of finds recovered from flotation will help in understanding the nature of the sample's context. At times, the sample may produce surprising results: for example, the flotation of certain contexts at Corinth has recovered chance finds of metal objects, including a lead seal and coins.

1.The most important step in preparing for water flotation is to place the small sieve in front of the barrel; if the sieve is not placed properly, all of the small residue will be lost. The small residue should never be touched by hand, as doing so can damage carbonized seeds or charcoal pieces.

2. Adjust the net to fit the barrel properly. Without the net, the soil will fall into the barrel and all of the data will be lost.

3. Check how many liters are in the sample and record this number in the SIZE (in L) field on the SAMPLE SHEET. Measuring the sample's volume is necessary to calculate the percentage of the context that was taken as a sample. Record the weight of the sample on the NOTES field of the SAMPLE SHEET if asked to do so by the Director of Excavations.

4. Pour the sample into the water. Wash the sample by stirring it until all the mud disappears. Any pieces that float should pass into the small sieve.

5. Allow the sample to dry. Do not attempt to sort the sample while it is still wet, as certain microfauna, such as fish bones, will remain attached to the wet soil.

6. Record any observations made during the water-flotation process (e.g. visible seeds, no visible seeds, half bits of charcoal, etc.). These notes will be important for gaining a general understanding of the context.

7. Place the small residue and its identification data on a paper towel and allow it to dry. Once the paper towel is dry, place the small residue in a bag and store it in the museum, together with the other light residue from the same context. A palaeobotanist or the charcoal expert will analyze the small residue once the flotation is complete.

8. When sorting the finds, use tweezers to separate the finds into different categories. Seeds found during sorting should be stored in plastic bags. All other finds from a single sample should be stored in a cardboard box that is labeled on the outside with the context number—do not store the finds separated by species (e.g. all of the fish bones together). Finds from each individual sample taken from a context are stored together, as are all samples from the same context.

During the flotation process, the barrel must be cleaned as often as possible—usually after about 10 samples have been processed. Every part of the water sieve must be kept clean. If the sieve is not cleaned regularly, accumulated mud will prevent the system from operating properly and risk contaminating the samples. At the end of the season, be sure to clean the water sieve thoroughly one final time.

2.6.1. Completing the Sample Recording Sheet

2.6.1.1. *Title Tag, Context Number, and Chronological Range*

Enter the TITLE TAG (see §6.2.1) and CONTEXT NUMBER of the context being sampled. Later, complete the CHRONOLOGICAL RANGE OF CONTEXT field (see §6.2.2), marking which material was used to date the context. Samples do not receive a new unique number—they are assigned the same number as the context from which they are taken.

2.6.1.2. *Sample Number*

Note how many samples were taken from the context (e.g. SAMPLE NUMBER "1 of 4"). This information will be useful in situations where several samples are taken from the same context but are kept separate for comparative analysis (such as a large floor or a burial) (see §2.6).

2.6.1.3. *Coordinates, Elevations, and Dimensions*

Take measurements (in meters) of the location and size of the sample and enter this information into the COORDINATES OF SAMPLE (see §6.2.5), ELEVATIONS OF SAMPLE (see §6.2.3), and DIMENSIONS OF SAMPLE fields. These measurements are for the sample itself, not the context.

2.6.1.4. *Sample Taken from Plan or Section*

In the SAMPLE TAKEN FROM field, note whether the sample was taken from the plan (i.e. from above the context—this will be the norm) or from a section (i.e. the vertical face of a section, see §4.3).

2.6.1.5. *Amount and Volume of Sample*

Estimate the PERCENT OF CONTEXT sampled, the SIZE (IN L) of the sample, and the NUMBER OF CONTAINERS USED to take the sample (see §6.2.14 and §6.2.15). Use the number of containers to estimate the size of the sample.

2.6.1.6. *Methods and Conditions*

In the METHODS AND CONDITIONS field, briefly describe the methods used to collect the sample and the soil conditions (see §6.2.13).

2.6.1.7. *Inclusions*

List any INCLUSIONS IN THE CONTEXT being sampled, and explain why sampling to water-sieve the context would be valuable (e.g., presence of organics, carbon, shells, etc.) (see §6.2.9).

2.6.1.8. *Harris Matrix*

Copy the HARRIS MATRIX OF THE CONTEXT BEING SAMPLED from the appropriate context recording sheet to this SAMPLE SHEET.

2.6.1.9. *Reasons for Sampling Context*

In the REASONS FOR SAMPLING CONTEXT field, discuss the reasons this context is being sampled. For example, is there a reasonable amount of organic material or carbonized organics preserved in the context? Is the context particularly wet or waterlogged? Were other related contexts sampled and this sample was required for comparison? Is this sample taken from a floor near a hearth or a food preparation area?

2.6.1.10. *Specific Questions about Sample*

In the SPECIFIC QUESTIONS ABOUT SAMPLE field, describe any questions about this sample. For example, will frequent types of animal bone provide information about diet? Will any seeds recovered provide information about the environmental conditions or the farming practices in use when this context was deposited? Have a series of stratified floors been sampled to show continuity or change in diet over time? These will not be the only questions taken into account during the post-excavation analysis, but they will help any researchers who consult the records in the future understand why this sample was taken.

2.6.1.11. *Sketch Plan*

Draw a sketch of the context showing the location of the sample. The sketch does not have to be to scale, since a top plan of this context will have been drawn already. Note dimensions or coordinate points and draw a NORTH ARROW in the labeled box. If multiple samples are taken from the same context, include them all on the same sketch so that it is easy to determine from where they were taken in relation to each other. If a fill from a pit or well has been sampled, a sketch of the context will suffice.

3. FORMATION PROCESSES AND EXCAVATION OF SPECIFIC CONTEXTS

3.1. FLOORS

The term **floor** is reserved for a purposefully constructed, smoothed level in an interior or exterior space (Fig. 4). Floors are sometimes constructed using special materials such as plaster, mosaic, or stone slabs, and in these cases are immediately recognizable. More frequently, however, and particularly in domestic structures, floors are constructed with earth or clay that has been beaten to a flat and smooth surface. These floors are recognizable on the ground as a crust of hard-packed earth or clay, often with sherds or other artifacts lying flat on top of them. Some floors are necessarily smooth and level constructions, as they are the use surfaces of interior spaces. For this reason, it is typical to find a deposit of soil used as leveling fill immediately below a floor, deposited to create the level surface for the floor itself. It is unlikely that a floor would have stones, tiles, bones, or other objects sticking up and through it. In such a situation, either the context is not a floor, or the floor surface was abraded with use over time. The presence of a later floor resurfacing would be evidence for the latter situation.

Any floor built with special materials should be recorded as a structure (see §3.2 regarding surfaces treated as structures), as the fields on the STRUCTURE SHEET will most accurately record such features. A floor that is not built of these or other materials and is simply a crust of packed earth should be recorded as a deposit, as the fields on the DEPOSIT SHEET will most accurately describe this feature. This crust should be cleaned well before being excavated as its own context. The underlying fill should also be assigned its own context number. The process of cleaning and removing the top crust before the underlying fill must be repeated as often as is necessary until all phases of the floor and localized floor repairs are removed. In the case of repairs, the repaired part must be recorded and removed separately from the original floor—each human action must be assigned its own context number.

Figure 4. Photo of a clay floor bounded by two walls, cut by a later pit in the background. Photo A. Carter

If objects are found resting on the floor (i.e. they have not been disturbed since their deposition), this assemblage must be assigned its own context number, as these objects were deposited at a different moment in time from both the construction of the floor and the deposition of the fill that covered the floor (see §8.7).

3.2. SURFACES

The term **surface** refers to a purposefully constructed exterior space that would have been exposed to the elements (Fig. 5). A surface might be, for example, an open-air interior courtyard or the surface of an animal pen or a yard used as a work area. Surfaces can be made of packed earth and/or supplemented with pebbles or crushed ceramics. If a substantial number of pebbles and cobbles are used in the surface, the decision may be made to record it using a STRUCTURE SHEET.

Figure 5. Surface of a central courtyard in a Byzantine house. Photo A. Carter

Exterior surfaces that are exposed to the elements—as well as human and animal foot traffic—most certainly will undergo a series of resurfacings and repairs. Once the surface is damaged, foot traffic and erosion gradually remove the hard trodden surface in this spot. Further erosion can create a depression in the damaged area that, in turn, will collect rainwash, silt, and windborne debris. Together these actions create a surface with a series of small depressions filled with silt, pebbles, and other debris that can be distinguished from the rest of the surface in the field. These silted-in depressions may be patched by a dump of earth and other materials that are packed down, recreating a relatively level surface. After years of use, an exterior surface will comprise a patchwork of depressions and repairs and possibly a series of partial or total resurfacings.

For each excavated surface, any damaged portion of the surface and surface repair(s) must be identified, isolated, and excavated individually using a DEPOSIT SHEET. Surfaces are generally recorded as deposits (see above for exception). They should be 100 percent dry sieved and possibly sampled for water floatation.

3.3. ROADS

Roads are distinguishable in the field by their very compact surfaces, their linear nature, their relationship to other roads and structures, and the fact that they are usually "metaled" unless they are built of stone slabs. The term **road metal** refers to a road surface constructed with crushed stone, gravel, or pebbles. Potholes and wheel ruts may also be preserved on the surface of roads.

A road that is built of stone paving should be recorded with a STRUCTURE SHEET, and a metaled road with a DEPOSIT SHEET. As with other surfaces (§3.2), repairs and repavings/resurfacings are each assigned individual context numbers. They are usually recorded as deposits, but sometimes they are recorded as cuts instead (e.g. wheel ruts or other disturbed areas on the road). Roads must be 100 percent dry sieved and sampled for water sieving. However, since traffic on a road may have damaged or destroyed any organics that would be recovered by water flotation, it may be useful to float a test sample of road material in the field before sampling more widely.

3.4. FOUNDATION TRENCHES

Wall construction techniques vary from period to period at Corinth. In some periods, the builders first dug a trench that was to be the same dimensions as the wall, then built the foundations of the wall inside this trench. When the foundations were laid, the gaps in the foundation trench were backfilled on one or both sides of the foundations, and the wall superstructure was built upon these foundations (Fig. 6). Backfilled gaps will typically be less compact than the soil into which the trench was dug, and they will typically extend 10–40 cm out from each wall face. Like pit fills, lenses of fill inside a foundation trench may not have been deposited in regular horizontal layers. If backfill from the original excavation of the wall was dumped into the foundation trench in a series of dumping actions, the fills might settle against the cut of the foundation trench, rather than lie horizontally. It is also likely that foundation trench fills will not be uniform along the entire length of a wall. This is particularly true for long walls, as the backfill may simply be composed of whatever soils into which the trench was dug, and these soils will have varied along the length of the wall. In the case of a site with multiple terraces, the foundation trenches of some walls dug may be dug to different depths on either side of the wall.

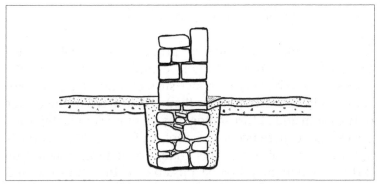

Figure 6. Wall with foundation trench with multiple fills, in section. Drawing J. Herbst

Not every wall, however, will have a foundation trench. Some foundations are constructed by placing stones or a mix of rubble and mortar into the foundation trench, completely filling the cut (Fig. 7). In this case, there would be no later backfilling of gaps in the foundation trench, since no gaps were left during construction. Such a construction technique does not usually leave a perceptible cut, but there will likely be a noticeable change in construction technique between the wall foundation and superstructure. This change allows the excavator to reconstruct the surface into which the foundations were laid, and thereby determine relative dating and establish stratigraphic relationships. Walls built directly on top of earlier walls also may lack foundation trenches, as they were never founded in the ground; still, it is likely that there will be a perceptible difference in the construction of the two phases of the wall.

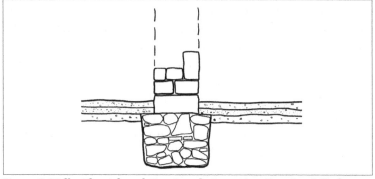

Figure 7. Wall without foundation trench, in section. Drawing J. Herbst

There are some site formation processes that make identifying a foundation trench more complicated. For example, floors tend to be very compact surfaces; however, they are compact because they are walked upon. Areas in the center of the room and at thresholds may be more compacted than areas that experienced less foot traffic, such as corners and the bases of walls. This change in compaction will be diffuse, and it may not be possible to find the true and continuous cut of the foundation trench in this scenario. Natural factors may also complicate matters. Roots tend to take the path of least resistance in their growth: they regularly are found at interfaces between cuts and fills, and they are also common along the interface between soil and a built structure (i.e. a wall and the soil abutting it). A very narrow strip of less compact soil running along a wall is more likely to be the result of root action than the top of a foundation trench. Water running down the exterior face of a wall also may erode or disturb the soil there and give the impression of a foundation trench. In both cases, careful excavation will show that what was initially interpreted as a cut does not continue into the underlying soil contexts. Finally, as with any less compact soils that fill cuts, loose fill in a foundation trench may settle over time and lead to settling in the layers of the fill or floor above. This will cause a change in elevation across the surface of the fill or floor, dipping down next to the wall. But as with the previous two examples, it will not be possible to find the true cut of the foundation trench in the slumped fill or floor.

Foundation trench fills must be carefully excavated (Figs. 8 and 9) and 100 percent dry sieved. Each lens of fill must be assigned its own context number, as foundation trenches can provide a secure date for the construction of walls. If a trench is too narrow to dig all the way to the base, the excavation of the fill(s) within it must be stopped arbitrarily until the surrounding soil can be excavated to a depth that allows digging to continue inside the trench. If there is no foundation trench and instead the wall foundation completely fills the cut, there is a risk of contamination as excavation of the surrounding floors and fills proceeds. A skin balk (see §2.4.1) should be left against the face of the wall foundation to prevent any material from the later foundation from contaminating the earlier surrounding deposits.

Figure 8. Foundation trench prior to excavation. Photo A. Carter

Figure 9. Foundation trench with top lens of fill removed. Photo A. Carter

3.5. ROBBING TRENCHES

A robbing trench may be created after a wall has gone out of use. The stones of the wall and sometimes even the foundations may be robbed (i.e. removed) to build a new structure. Robbing trenches are common features, as it is easier to rob out a preexisting wall than to quarry new building material. Robbing trenches are recognizable during an excavation as roughly linear features that are often related to still-existing walls. The fill inside the robbing trench is usually less compact that the fill it cuts; however, this is not always the case, as the compaction of the fill is dependent upon the composition of the soil being used as backfill (e.g. clayey soil will be more compact than sandy or silty soil once it fills the trench). Sometimes the robbing trench was backfilled immediately after the robbing took place, particularly in an area of continuous building activity and use of space, where large open trenches would be a hazard. In other cases, the trench may have been left open for a period of time before it was backfilled. **Silting**, or the slumping of the sides of the cut and erosional deposition at the bottom of the trench under the backfill, would be evidence of the latter situation. Robbing trenches that were left open for a period of time might suggest a period of abandonment for that part of the site.

Fig. 10 illustrates the phases of abandonment and robbing of a wall in section: (a) the wall in use; (b) the wall after the structure has gone out of use: part of the upper wall has collapsed and debris has fallen from the structure to lie against the wall on both sides; (c) further degradation of the wall, with layers of fill accumulating above it and leaving a noticeable hump in section; and (d) the removal of the wall and its foundation, and therefore the creation of a robbing trench. Note that in Fig. 10d, the robbing trench is narrower than the original foundation trench, and so it did not completely remove the foundation trench fill (see Fig. 11). A careful excavator, therefore, would still be able to identify and excavate the original foundation trench fill despite the robbing activity. A robbing trench should be

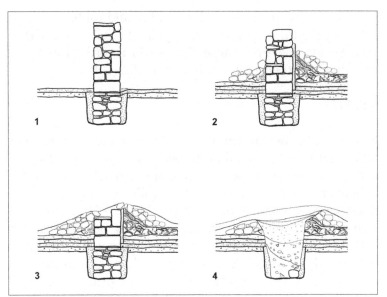

Figure 10. Four stages of the creation of a robbing trench, in section. Drawing J. Herbst

Figure 11. Robbing trench post-excavation, showing preserved foundation trench. Photo A. Carter

31

recorded with a CUT SHEET, foundation and robbing trench fills with multiple DEPOSIT SHEETS, and the wall with a STRUCTURE SHEET. Together, these sheets will record all of these activities and their relationships (see §6.2–6.4).

3.6. PITS

Pits are of particular importance because they are discrete units that usually contain dumped material, which may be useful for dating purposes. They are also sources of valuable microfaunal data that may be collected through water flotation (see §2.6). Pits are typically circular or oval in shape, and they can be recognized easily because the fill within the cut is different from the soil into which the pit is cut. Usually the pit fill is less compact than the surrounding deposits, and it may contain different inclusions (although this is not always the case). As with foundation and robbing trench fills, loose pit fills can settle over time, creating a slumping of the deposits that cover them (see §3.4 and 3.5). This makes finding the cut of the pit more complicated, as the depression caused by the settling of the deposits overlying the pit can be mistaken for the pit itself.

The full extent of the pit cut must be revealed before the fills inside are excavated. If the pit cut is irregular in shape, it may have been truncated by later action; if this is the case, the later deposits must be removed before the pit fills are excavated. Unless it is logistically impossible or unsafe to do so, it is good practice to section the fills of a pit (see §2.4.3 and 4.3). This will help ensure that even very subtle changes between fill contexts are observed both in plan and in section, and that the stratification of the pit fills are fully understood. Sectioning can also allow for more complex environmental sampling. Pits should be 100 percent dry sieved and sampled for water floatation.

3.7. WELLS

At Corinth, wells are cut into bedrock or soil and often have a wellhead built of stones. The cuts of wells have straight sides, and they are generally circular in plan, very deep, and usually with rough-hewn handholds. They are dug in order to reach the natural water table. Wells are distinguishable from another common feature at Corinth: the manhole that connects down to a water channel, which is a part of the water supply system.

Usually if a well went out of use but later activity continued to take place in the same area, the well was used as a rubbish dump and then backfilled (often quickly) to create a level surface with the ground soon after its abandonment. When the fills of a well are removed, it is useful to establish an elevation point at the mouth of the well. This point can be used to measure the depths of the fills within the shaft using a tape measure if and when it becomes impossible to use the total station as the depth inside increases. All attempts should be made to identify the stratigraphy of different fills within the well shaft and to excavate them in stratigraphic sequence. However, this may not be possible if the well is very deep, has been subjected to substantial sorting by the action of the water inside, or contains a single massive backfill dumped inside. In these cases, the fill inside the shaft should be removed in 10-cm units, assigning a unique context number to each fill within the well. The fills should be 100 percent dry sieved, and samples must be taken for flotation.

3.8. LEVELING AND DUMPED FILLS

At a site with multiple occupation phases, each new phase may be built on the remains of the previous phase. Elements of the earlier phases might be reused (e.g. walls may be robbed, new phases of walls may be built on top of earlier walls, roads may be resurfaced, or thresholds may be raised). In some areas, however, the new occupants may have created a level and uninterrupted surface on which to lay floors and surfaces and construct new buildings. Oftentimes in these instances, episodes of leveling and terracing to create the new higher surface (i.e. **leveling fill**) are preserved. These episodes can be minor, as when a floor

33

is abraded and goes out of use: in this situation, leveling fill may be spread over the floor and a new floor established above this. Leveling also can be a more massive operation, such as at sites built on a slope, where the slope is terraced to maximize the potential for flat spaces (e.g. in the later Forum area). In the case of terracing, it is common in Greece to encounter terrace walls that support the leveled soil from the side. These are typical features of both ancient and modern agriculture, as well as urban areas. Leveling fills are distinguishable in the field by their association with later floors or structures and the heterogeneous and poorly sorted nature of their inclusions (see §6.2.9). Dumped fills may be found in association with surfaces or leveling operations, and they are distinguishable by the fact that they are composed of random materials and fill uneven depressions. A **dumped fill** may be a **midden** (or rubbish heap), but it is distinguished by the fact that it was not dumped in order to create a level surface.

4. FIELD DRAWINGS

The site architect is responsible for producing professional plans of the excavation and the archaeological site as a whole. Professional drawings of specific features will be produced throughout the course of the season. However, supervisors will be doing the majority of the drawing in the field on a daily basis, drawing each context before it is excavated and any vertical sections, as appropriate.

4.1. DRAWING CONVENTIONS

Consistency is very important in an open-area excavation, as many different hands will be drawing contexts that are related. For this reason, conventions have been developed that must be followed in all field drawings. The symbols below (Fig. 12) have been chosen because they are simple, naturalistic, and immediately comprehensible, so a key is not necessary for every drawing. The conventions rely heavily on various line weights and types. Proper line weight is a helpful communication tool that can change the emphasis and meaning of a drawing, as well as give it a richness that makes it more understandable. In general, heavier line weights are used for harder materials, taller features, man-made edges, well-defined edges, and entities the supervisor wants to emphasize (such as the edge of deposit that is being currently excavated). Poorly preserved faces, indefinite edges, and shallow, gradual changes should be drawn more delicately. Dashed and center lines (line–dash-line) have specific meanings. Dotted and other styled lines can be cautiously employed for various uses, but they must be clearly labeled in each drawing.

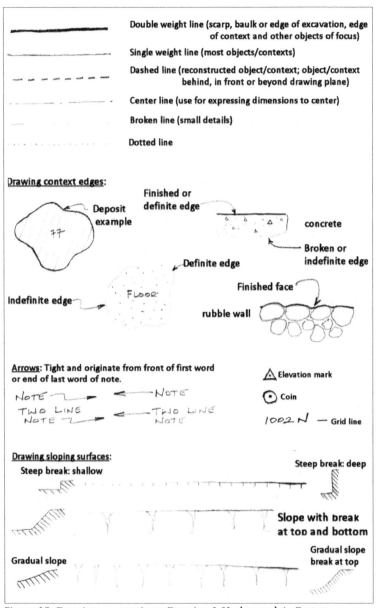

Figure 12. Drawing conventions. Drawing J. Herbst and A. Carter

4.2. TOP PLANS

A top plan is a "bird's-eye view" of the context being recorded **before** it is excavated. A top plan must be drawn in the field at the time of excavation for every recorded context—deposits, cuts, and structures all require top plans. Top plans should be large enough to include the position and limits of the context and show how the context is related to other features, such as walls, pits, significant cuts, changes in slope or elevation, distinct deposits, etc. The context being drawn and any other related features must all be clearly labeled. Elevations, including the findspots of objects such as coins and concentrations of pottery, should also be marked.

The total station may be used to establish the basic location of a context and to identify temporary points from which to measure within the context on the DRAWING SHEET. However, the total station must not be used to "draw" the context. Top plans that are based on a series of total station points are simply polygons and are not a true reflection of the shape or boundaries of the context. The position and shape of the context in the top plan should be accurate and carefully measured using the temporary points, but also drawn with freehand based on those measurements (see §4.4 for instructions on laying out a right angle as an aid for producing measured drawings.)

Unless the area being recorded is particularly large or small, a scale of 1:50 should be uniformly used on all top plans. A scale ruler should be used in the field for top plans. Grid labels (easting and northing axes) must be labeled at the edges of the grid paper so as to allow for easy comparison between any two or more plans. Once a drawing that accurately shows all the key elements (described above) has been produced, it can be used as a template for future top plans of contexts in this area. While it is initially time-consuming to produce a drawing that reflects all the meaningful features in the area being excavated, doing so allows future scholars to immediately understand the relationships between the individual recorded context and the contexts immediately around it.

On the gridded DRAWING SHEET, write the AREA of excavation (e.g. South Stoa), the CONTEXT number, the supervisor's name (next to DRAWN BY), the DATE, and the SCALE in the fields provided. Using a compass, draw a north arrow here as well. If more than one sheet of grid paper is needed to draw the context, fill in "Page 1 of X," "2 of X," etc., on the plan. Include top elevations in the drawing following the convention described above in §4.1 (do not include bottom elevations). Multiple top elevations may be shown on each top plan to fully express the nature of the top surface of the context. The bottom of the context will be reflected in the next top plan of the area or, if excavation does not continue in that area, in the final top plan. Final top plans are created following the same principles at the end of the excavation season by each team to show the work that was done. The plans are supplemented with photography (see §5) and, at Corinth, photogrammetry and final drawings by the site architect.

If coins are found in a deposit, use the measurements taken with the total station to label their exact findspot on the top plan for that context. These locations do not need to appear in future plans.

4.3. VERTICAL SECTIONS

A **vertical section** (or cross section) is a vertical slice through the site, revealing strata that can then be viewed from the side (see §2.4.3 for discussion). When systematically used with top plans, a vertical section is a useful visual tool for showing stratigraphic relationships as they are excavated. In most cases in an open-area excavation, it is only possible to draw a section after the contexts have been excavated; this is done using the top and bottom elevations and the top plans that were created for each individual context. In this case, the vertical section is reconstructed, since it attempts to reconstruct the site stratification using measurements after excavation is complete. As a rule, reconstructed sections should be draw any time the supervisor feels that a visual illustration of the vertical sequence will assist later scholars in understanding the stratigraphy of a part of the site. Because each context is recorded and drawn individually, sections can be reconstructed wherever they are needed on site. When reconstructing a section, a note should be made on all applicable context recording sheets by checking the SECTION box in the DRAWINGS field. Make a careful note on the drawing itself, as well as in the NOTES field, about where the section was reconstructed (northing and easting coordinates) and which direction the section faces.

If a series of contexts are sectioned during excavation (e.g. if multiple fills inside a pit are half-sectioned), then a section must be drawn of the vertical scarp that was created by this excavation technique. The vertical edges of the excavation might also require section drawings. In a careful excavation, however, many stratigraphic changes are easier to perceive horizontally than vertically; thus, the section should not be allowed to dictate how the surrounding areas are excavated. It should never be assumed that a section will reveal everything about the surrounding area. These kinds of sections should be drawn on site using measurements taken in the field with the total station, measuring tapes, and a plumb bob. The vertical section must always be scraped and swept down before being drawn.

A note should be made on all applicable context sheets that a vertical section has been drawn.

4.4. MEASURING OFF THE GRID AND LAYING OUT A RIGHT ANGLE

The total station is often used to establish reference points (which are marked on the ground with nails and labels) in and around the excavation area. It should also be used when drawing top plans. Measuring tapes can be laid between reference points to create a measured line on a known grid line. A perpendicular line can be established using the total station or a geometric calculation (see below). With a second measuring tape laid along the perpendicular line, very accurate measurements can be taken for any point that must be located in space on the grid (Fig. 13).

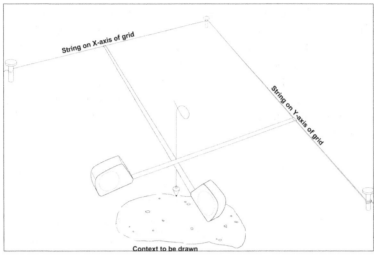

Figure 13. A quick way to take accurate measurements off the grid. Drawing J. Herbst

The hypotenuse of a right triangle, in which the adjacent sides equal the integer side, is $\sqrt{2}$ or 1.4142. Thus if a 1-x-1-m square is laid out, the diagonals will measure 1.4142 m. This formula allows a line to be established perpendicular to the grid line without using the total station.This formula can be adjusted to accommodate any size excavation square by multiplying the value $\sqrt{2}$ by the desired length of the sides:

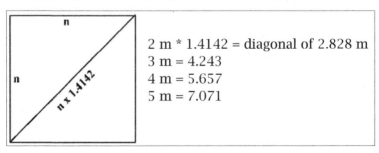

2 m * 1.4142 = diagonal of 2.828 m
3 m = 4.243
4 m = 5.657
5 m = 7.071

5. SITE PHOTOGRAPHS

Digital photographs must be taken before and after each context is excavated in order to fully document the excavation.

Additional photographs must be taken of floors and surfaces, postholes, pits, wellheads, robbing and foundation trenches, pipes and pipe trenches, drainage channels, graves ([a] the top and bottom of the cut, and [b] the skeleton before removal), structures ([a] when the tops are first revealed, and [b] later when fully revealed), and any structure that will be removed.

Photographs must be taken before these features are excavated. It is the responsibility of everyone on site to ensure that this happens. Additional photographs must be taken of complete vessels and any other finds that will be inventoried in the museum as they are revealed in situ, as well as any unusual soil features. If it is unclear whether a photo should be taken, consult with the Field Director. The Field Director is responsible for taking photographs, uploading digital images to the database, and noting photograph numbers on appropriate recording sheets. At Corinth, a continuous sequence of numbers is used for digital photos; the Field Director should check to see which number sequences to use.

Before a photograph is taken, the area must be swept and all extraneous tools and equipment removed from the field of view. Photographs should illustrate the context being recorded and its relationship to surrounding contexts and features. Sometimes multiple photographs are needed to accomplish this aim. **A scaled north arrow is used in all photographs.**

6. FIELD RECORDING PROCEDURES

There are three types of contexts: deposits, structures, and cuts. Each type of context has its own recording sheet that documents the information relevant to that specific context. Each sheet, however, shares certain fields, and therefore the descriptions below on how to fill out these common fields are useful for all recording sheets. Note that each field on every type of recording sheet can be referenced back to this section and it should be consulted whenever questions arise. Specific fields for each type of context are also discussed in this section.

All the Corinth Excavations' records are kept together in one notebook, rather than requiring students to maintain their own set of records. The paper records made in the field are transferred to a computer database at the end of each day, with the goal being that all the records will be fully digitized and searchable at the end of the excavations.

The recording sheets are made up of two types of fields: more "objective" pull-down menus, and more "subjective," less structured, free-text fields. The pull-down menus require a structured response based on the options listed in the sections below. If there truly are no appropriate options in a pull-down menu, a subjective textual response may be provided in the NOTES field (see §6.2.18). Keep in mind that there must be a balance between structure (which aids in searching, indexing, and creating relationships and associations) and precision (accurately defining the characteristics of a context). Ultimately all observations in the field are interpretive, but using a standardized system of recording helps make the data that is produces as useful as possible.

All excavation sheets must be written in pen. Even if the interpretation of the context is later changed, it is important to have a record of the first impressions of the context. Later interpretations can be added easily to the context recording sheet and the database by noting the date and the new explanation.

6.1. THE CONTEXT REGISTER

To prevent the same context number from being assigned to more than one context—or a number in the sequence from being skipped—**the context number must be registered before the context can be recorded.** The context register is kept by the Field Director. For the purpose of the register, the description of the context is not critical, but it should be intelligible to anyone consulting the register during the excavation season. It does not need to match the TITLE TAG (see §6.2.1) for that context.

The Lot Number **and** Chronological Range **fields are filled in post-excavation.**

6.2. DEPOSITS

Deposits are positive contexts (as opposed to cuts) and are not built features (as opposed to structures). Most contexts are deposits. Pit fills, surfaces, agricultural plow zones, and natural events like flood wash and grave fills are all examples of deposits. Because of the dynamic process of site formation and the fact that deposits may accumulate gradually over time and/or be exposed to the elements when they are on the surface, it is to be expected that the edges of a deposit naturally will come to a feathered edge except when the deposit fills a cut. If a deposit has a hard edge or boundary (either curved or straight), it is essential to rule out the possibility of a later cut interrupting the deposit before excavating the deposit. Neglecting to do so may result in deposits being excavated out of stratigraphic order.

6.2.1. Title Tag

The TITLE TAG is the essential summary of the context, and the description in this field should be kept short and to the point (not more than 10 words). Use keywords and phrases that not only describe the deposit, but also define it. The description of the TITLE TAG can be composed out of the field—and it can be changed later—as it is possible that a full understanding of the deposit will only be possible after the finds are analyzed and the deposit is incorporated into the Harris Matrix. In other words, the TITLE TAG field can be modified if new information allows for a more precise interpretation later. This field is most useful as a quick reference tool.

A good TITLE TAG should describe the defining characteristics of the context and not simply reference other contexts. If referencing a related context, use its TITLE TAG in a shortened form and **do not reference** CONTEXT NUMBERS **unless they are wall numbers.** Do not mention the chronological date of the context, as this information will appear in the CHRONOLOGICAL RANGE field, although it may be important to note earlier or later relative phases (i.e. above and below the context). Likewise, avoid referencing any database field (COLOR, COMPOSITION, COMPACTION, SORTING, etc.) that has a pull-down menu unless you it is absolutely definitive for the context (i.e. there is nothing else that can be written about it to define it). Avoid abbreviations, and **list the most important and definitive words first.**

Here are some examples of good and bad title tags:

Good TITLE TAG	Bad TITLE TAG
Pit fill, third deposit from top Dumped fill Agricultural zone cut by modern plow furrows Ashy fill of small pit N–S partition wall E–W property boundary wall Destruction debris: tile scatter Floor of packed earth Leveling fill below clay floor Exterior surface repair Robbing trench fill of wall 5604 Well fill, tenth deposit from top Floor over wall 5604 Floor cut by foundation trench of wall 5604 Natural deposit	Fill of orange tree pit, pit cut = context 9 [do not reference other context numbers except walls] Third deposit of fill in pit [use the most important words first (e.g. "pit")] Reddish soil E of context 43 ["reddish" will appear elsewhere on the recording sheet; "soil" is vague; another context is referenced; and the title tag does not convey the essence, function, or formation of the deposit] Middle Roman destruction debris [chronological range will appear elsewhere on the recording sheet] Fill of well south of 18 [use the most important words first (e.g. "well"); "south of 18" is vague and conveys no essential information] Silty soil 10 m east of wall 5302 [composition of the soil will appear elsewhere on the recording sheet; a wall number is referenced, but it is unclear if the deposit and the wall have a direct relationship or if the wall is simply a numbered feature west of the context being recorded] Northern floor patch [it is unclear what is south of this floor patch, so "northern" should be omitted in this example]

6.2.2. Chronological Range

The CHRONOLOGICAL RANGE field, which appears on all context recording sheets, can only be filled in after all the pottery has been read and recorded, all the coins have been read by the numismatist and recorded, the Harris Matrix has been completed, and all other finds that could potentially affect the date of the context have been examined in the museum. **Record the latest date supplied by all the evidence collected for the context.** For example, if a context contains pottery dating to the 4th century A.D. as well as a 6th century A.D. coin, the first assessment of the date of the context would be the 6th century A.D. based on material culture present in the context. However, if a floor surface dated to the middle of the 7th century A.D. is revealed below this hypothetical context, the chronological range for the earlier context with the 6th-century coin must be amended to show that it, too, must date to the middle of the 7th century or later, as it must have been deposited after the floor went out of use. This chronological field should be updated any time the stratigraphic sequence impacts the dating of contexts based on relationships established with the Harris Matrix. On the context recording sheet and in the database, note which body of evidence was used to date the context in the DATED BY field: pottery, coin, or other (which could be a find [in this case, provide a description] or a stratigraphic relationship). Pottery dates are recorded separately in the pottery fields in the database and should never be changed once the pottery has been dated.

The final date of a context is not normally assigned until near the end of the excavation because it requires all relevant information to be assessed.

6.2.3. Elevations

ELEVATIONS must be taken on the top surface of every context excavated. The highest of the top elevations is entered in the TOP field on the recording sheet, but if the context is uneven, all other elevations should be recorded on the top plan (see §4.2). Once the context has been excavated and recorded, several representative elevations should be taken on the surface revealed by the removal of the context. The lowest of these elevations should be entered in the BOTTOM field on the recording sheet. All additional elevations should be recorded in the NOTES field (see §6.2.18).

6.2.4. Slope Down To and Slope Degree

By comparing the different elevations taken on the top surface of each context, it will be possible to determine whether the surface slopes down toward any particular cardinal direction (N, NE, E, SE, S, etc.)—enter this information in the SLOPE DOWN TO field. The SLOPE DEGREE is an estimate of the degree to which the top surface slopes. Choose from the following options:

SLOPE DOWN TO	SLOPE DEGREE
[cardinal direction]	Level
	Slight
	Moderate
	Steep
	Vertical
	Uneven

6.2.5. Coordinates

Based on the northing and easting coordinates taken with the total station and confirmed by measuring temporary points by hand, the size and shape of the context allow for a determination of the greatest extents of the context to the north, south, east, and west. The COORDINATES field is used to record the greatest extent of the context and its location. An accurately measured top plan will be useful here, as these coordinates ideally should be taken from it.

6.2.6. Color

Ideally the soil should be moist when its color is assessed; therefore, it is best to describe the soil when it is fresh during excavation. If the deposit is shallow and dry at the time of excavation, it should be sprayed so that the true color is restored. Describing soil color is a potentially subjective process; however, using a standard set of terms helps to make the procedure more structured. It is much more important to describe the color of a deposit in order to distinguish it from surrounding contexts than it is to analyze the color down to the individual particle level.

Complete the Color fields by choosing from the terms below (from Spence [1994: Section 3.1.1.2] and the Munsell Soil Color Charts [Munsell Color 1994]). There are three components to describing soil color: a MODIFIER, HUE, and COLOR. Choose only one term for each component:

MODIFIER	HUE	COLOR
Light	Brownish	Black
Dark	Greenish	Brown
Very Dark	Greyish	Green
	Pinkish	Grey
	Reddish	Pink
	Yellowish	Red
		White
		Yellow
		Mixed*

*Only select "Mixed" in the COLOR field if the soil is not uniform in color, then make sure to describe the different colors in the NOTES field (see §6.2.18). "Mixed," as a rule, should be reserved only for soils that truly are mixed in color and have more than one distinct color component; mixed soils will appear patchy and yet be definitively part of the same context.

6.2.7. Composition

All soils will be comprised of a combination of sand, silt, or clay. Sand feels gritty, and the individual grains are visible to the naked eye. Silt is smooth and slippery to the touch when wet and like fine powder when dry; the individual particles are much smaller than those of sand and can be seen only with the aid of a microscope. Clay is sticky and plastic when wet and extremely hard and compact when dry; the individual particles are extremely small and can only be seen with the aid of an electron microscope. Soil must be touched and handled in order for its composition to be described.

As a supervisor, it is ideal to record the soil composition during excavation by grabbing a handful of soil and discussing the properties of the soil with the excavator.

The COMPOSITION field asks for the major element in a deposit. The soil should be carefully inspected, but it is unhelpful to attempt to calculate percentages of different soil components in the field without the aid of a microscope and a complex sampling strategy, as this will most likely be an inaccurate assessment of the micro-composition of the soil and give a false sense of the method used to determine soil composition. Until a better method is developed, one of the following descriptive options must be chosen:

<u>COMPOSITION</u>
Coarse sand
Fine sand
Silty sand
Clayey sand
Silt
Sandy silt
Clayey silt
Clay
Sandy clay
Silty clay
Mixed*

*The same guidelines for selcting "Mixed" for the COLOR field apply to the COMPOSITION field.

6.2.8. Compaction

The COMPACTION field describes the degree of compaction of the soil in a deposit. The compaction of the soil can only be determined through communication between the supervisor and the excavator. Supervisors are encouraged to participate in the excavation of deposits with the aid of the excavators, as with all other aspects of soil description.

The terms used to describe soil compaction are based in part on the composition of the soil (Fig. 14); therefore, the composition must be described before the compaction.

COMPACTION	SEDIMENT	DEFINITION TYPE
Strongly cemented	Coarse-grained	Cannot be broken with hands.
Weakly cemented		Pick removes sediment in lumps which can be broken with hands.
Compact		Requires pick for excavation
Loose		Can be excavated with trowel
Hard	Fine-grained	Brittle or very tough.
Firm		Molded by strong finger pressure
Soft		Easily molded with fingers
Very Soft		Non-plastic, crumbles in fingers

Figure 14. Chart for describing soil compaction. After Spence 1994

6.2.9. Inclusions

Inclusions are any material in the soil that is not soil (i.e. ceramic sherds, glass fragments, stones, shell, bone and other organics like ash, carbon or land shells, plaster fragments, mud brick fragments, tile [small or large fragments], and other building materials). Small finds like metal objects will be described in detail during the museum inventorying processes, so it is unnecessary to list small finds as inclusions in this field. List all inclusions that are present and estimate the percentage of total inclusions in the soil (Fig. 15). A more detailed description of inclusions may be included in the NOTES field (see §6.2.18). In particular, it is important to describe all types of inclusions that are very frequent, as well as those that are infrequent.

Size is not a field on the DEPOSIT SHEET (or in the database), but it should be incorporated into the description of inclusions in the INCLUSIONS field. Describe the size of the **primary inclusions** in the deposit. For stones, use the chart in Fig. 17 to standardize the vocabulary of the description. For other inclusions, it is more useful to provide average dimensions (in meters).

Shape and roundness is likewise not a field on the DEPOSIT SHEET (or in the database), but it should be incorporated into the description of inclusions in the INCLUSIONS field. Using Fig. 18 as a guide, describe the shape and roundness of stone inclusions. This information helps to determine the nature and origin of the deposit.

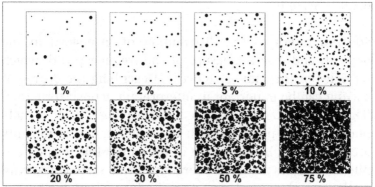

Figure 15. Estimated percentage of inclusions in soil composition.
Drawing J. Herbst, after Hodgson 1974

Fine Pebbles	0.002-0.006 m
Medium Pebbles	0.006-0.020 m
Coarse Pebbles	0.020-0.060 m
Cobbles	0.060-0.200 m
Boulders	>0.200 m

Figure 16. Modified Wentworth Scale for describing the
size of stones.

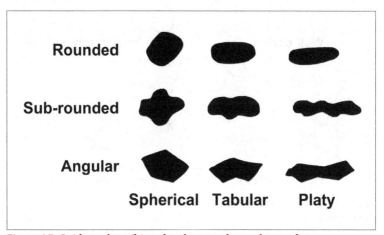

Figure 17. Guide to describing the shape and roundness of stones.
Drawing J. Herbst

6.2.9.1. *Sorting*

SORTING refers to the distribution of inclusions in the deposit, and it is a measure of the frequency with which particles of the same size occur. Describing the degree of sorting can be important in interpreting deposit formation (Fig. 18). For example, dumped and leveling fills are usually poorly or very poorly sorted; water-laid natural sediments are well-sorted by the action of the water; fills inside deep pits or trenches may be moderately or well sorted by gravity as they are deposited; and deposits formed gradually over time (as may happen when a mud brick building is abandoned and left to decay) may have a more complex particle distribution.

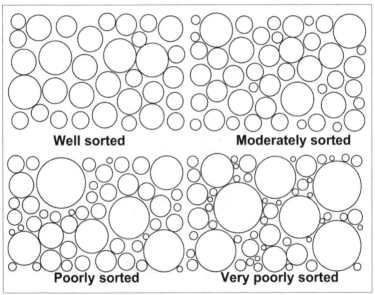

Figure 18. Chart for estimating the degree of sorting. Drawing J. Herbst, after Folk 1988

When describing the level of sorting of the inclusions in a deposit, choose from the following options: Well sorted, Moderately sorted, Poorly sorted, Very poorly sorted.

6.2.10. Harris Matrix and Stratigraphic Relationships

See §1.4 for an explanation of the principles behind the Harris Matrix. Use this field on the context recording sheets to begin assembling the overall Harris Matrix for the site by focusing on the context being recording (the center rectangle in Fig. 19), as well as any and all other contexts that are **physically related** (i.e. actually touching). This information is the foundation upon which a Harris Matrix of the site can be created to map chronological, rather than purely physical, relationships.

In the matrix, context numbers located **above the context being recorded** were deposited or created **later** in time. Context numbers located **below the context being recorded** were deposited or created **earlier** in time.

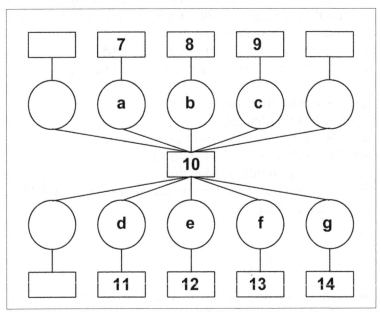

Figure 19. A modified Harris Matrix with hypothetical contexts. Drawing J. Herbst.

When the overall site Harris Matrix is composed, positive features (deposits, structures, skeletons, and discrete deposits of artifacts) will be represented as a context number inside a rectangle, as shown in Fig. 19, and negative features (cuts) as an oval. However, in the field version—which is a work in progress—all contexts besides the context being recorded will be represented as rectangles.

Use the **empty circles** incorporated into the lines connecting contexts to describe the physical characteristics and relationships between the contexts. This procedure is intended to be a means of recording why each context is recognized as distinct from its surrounding contexts and how each context physically relates to the others.

6.2.10.1. *Characteristics*

The CHARACTERISTICS field requires an explanation of why the context being recorded is considered a distinct unit and how it is different from the contexts around it. This text should take the form of simple comparisons based on observations made about soil color, composition, compaction, and inclusions. For the example matrix shown above (see §6.2.10), the CHARACTERISTICS field might read:

(a) 7 is harder than 10
(b) 8 is blacker than 10
(c) 9 is blacker and has fewer inclusions than 10
(d) 10 is softer and redder than 11
(e) 10 is very slightly redder than 12
(f) 10 is softer and redder and has more rounded pebble inclusions than 13
(g) 14 is a cut

6.2.10.2. *Relationships*

Use the RELATIONSHIPS field to record how the contexts in the Harris Matrix physically relate to each other. As explained in §1.4, there are only a few types of relationships that can exist between contexts. These relationships should be recorded in both this field and the appropriate database field; therefore, you must choose from the following options:

56

If the context being recorded is **earlier** than another context:

The context is **filled by** it
The context is **overlaid by** it
The context is **cut by** it

The context being recorded is **equal** to another context when it can be proven that a single context has been truncated by later action and now exists in two or more parts (i.e. separated by the later activity), or when a single context has been section-excavated in two or more parts, each with separate context numbers. When this is an equivalent relationship, write in the equivalent context number with an equal sign next to the central rectangle in the matrix.

If the context being recorded is **later than** another context:

The context is **laid on** it (e.g. dumped fills covering earlier deposits or fill inside the cut of a pit)
The context is **laid against** it (i.e. the boundary between the two is vertical)
The context **cuts** it

In the example matrix shown above (see §6.2.10), the RELATIONSHIPS field might read:

(a) 7 is laid on 10
(b) 8 is laid on 10
(c) 9 cuts 10
(d) 10 cuts 11
(e) 10 is laid on 12
(f) 10 is laid against 13
(g) 10 is laid on 14

The Harris Matrix RELATIONSHIPS field in the database will be used to generate a master matrix for the entire site, and therefore it is extremely important. The information entered into the database fields should be considered the final product of the Harris Matrix process that started in the field, and **it should be updated any time a new interpretation of stratigraphic relationships is made.**

6.2.11. Boundaries with Other Contexts

The BOUNDARIES WITH OTHER CONTEXTS field can only be completed when the context being recorded has been completely excavated. This field records the degree of change between the context being recorded and the context(s) revealed below it.

If more than one context is revealed below the one being recorded and they differ in how distinct they are from the context being recorded, leave this field blank and elaborate in the NOTES field (see §6.2.18).

BOUNDARIES WITH OTHER CONTEXTS

Sharp   the change is dramatic and very easy to see (i.e. a major change in color, texture, inclusions, or all of the above).

Clear   the change is clear, but not dramatic (i.e. a clear change in color, texture, or inclusions).

Diffuse   the change is not clear or easy to see, but it is perceived by a slight change in color, texture, or inclusions.

6.2.12. Formation/Interpretation

All archaeological deposits are a result of human or natural action. Understanding the nature of this action is integral to the understanding of overall site formation. Interpretations of the nature, function, and formation of the deposit are recorded in the FORMATION/INTERPRETATION field. This can be a straightforward procedure in cases where the nature of the context is obvious, such as when the context is a pit or foundation trench fill. In such cases, the formation of the deposit is immediately understandable—possibly even before the deposit has been excavated. In other cases, however, the nature of the deposit may be less readily understandable at the moment of excavation. For example, it might be difficult to determine whether a large deposit is dumped fill or leveling fill without fully excavating it first, examining the relationship of the deposit to other contexts in the Harris Matrix, and cataloguing the pottery and finds from the deposit.

While it is always best practice to record the initial field interpretation of the deposit, it is possible that the interpretation may change after all the data is considered post-excavation. It is acceptable to express doubt when recording the initial field interpretation by using phrases such as "deposit accumulated over a wall—degraded mud brick?," "possibly leveling fill or dumped fill," or "ashy fill— the remains of an outdoor cooking fire?" Honesty is always preferred in regard to the understanding of the nature and formation of a deposit, rather than attempting to force an interpretation with no evidence to support it. However, it is essential that an attempt be made to interpret the nature of the deposit, however tentative that interpretation may be. If data accumulated post-excavation suggest a more plausible interpretation, this field can be updated on the recording sheet and in the database so long as it is made clear that this is a later interpretation. The phrase "later interpretation" should be used or, alternatively, the new, later date and a new entry should be made in the NOTES field (see §6.2.18) to provide a detailed explanation justifying the new interpretation using specific pieces of data.

6.2.13. Method and Conditions

The METHOD AND CONDITIONS field should be completed with information about the tools used and the soil conditions experienced during excavation:

<u>**Tools used:**</u>
Small pick
Big pick,
Trowel
Wooden chopstick,
Broom
[etc.]

Soil Conditions:
Excavated Dry*
Excavated Moist

*"Dry" means truly parched soil that holds no moisture even under the surface exposed to the elements. If the deposit being recorded was exposed to the elements for a length of time (i.e. more than a few days), comment on how long this period of exposure lasted (e.g. 1 week, 2 weeks, since last excavation season, etc.). Mention if there was recent significant rainfall or if the soil was sprayed down with water prior to excavation.

6.2.14. Dry Sieving

In the DRY SIEVING field, indicate whether or not this deposit was dry sieved (see §2.5), the size of the mesh sieve that was used (at Corinth we typically use 5mm), and the percent of the total context that was sieved. The latter can be estimated by counting the number of buckets or wheelbarrows of soil that are removed during excavation and then calculating the ratio between those taken to the dump and those taken to be sieved.

6.2.15. Flotation Samples

In the FLOTATION SAMPLES field, indicate whether sample(s) for water flotation were taken from this deposit, the volume of the samples (in liters), and the percent of the context that this sample constitutes. If samples were taken, a SAMPLE SHEET must be completed (see §2.6.1).

6.2.16. Coins

Generally, information about inventoried objects will not be recorded in the field, but some information regarding coins must be recorded as each coin is uncovered. When a coin is found while excavating a context, immediately measure its coordinates using the total station, then mark the findspot on the top plan with these measurements, its elevation, and the word "Coin" written next to it. In the COINS field, list each coin with its elevation and leave a space, as each coin will be given a unique number in the museum that will need to be added in this space (e.g. 2008-178):

"Coin (87.23 El.): _____"

All coins are taken to the museum at the end of the day in individual paper envelopes. **On the outside of the envelope, record the area of excavation (e.g. "Nezi" or "N of Nezi"), the date, the context number, and the northing, easting, and elevation measurements from the total station. Draw an outline around the coin** on the outside of the envelope in pencil so that in the unlikely case that a coin is separated from its envelope, the two can be reunited later and the data recording its findspot is not lost. Coins found while sieving should also be brought to the museum packaged like this, but instead of noting the measurements of their findspot, write "from sieve."

6.2.17. Finds Collected

List the finds collected from each context in the FINDS COLLECTED field, along with general quantities of each category (e.g. glass [1 box], metal [1 bag], bone/shell [1 box], etc.). A list of all finds—regardless of whether they are being sent to the pot sheds or to the museum—should be present on every DEPOSIT SHEET. This is intended to be a safeguard against any finds being collected in the field and not subsequently catalogued post-excavation.

6.2.18. Notes

The NOTES field provides an opportunity to give an account in narrative form of any observations made about the deposit being recorded and any interpretations or questions raised about the deposit or other aspects of the excavation in general. It is perfectly acceptable to be repetitive here if it is necessary to emphasize salient points (i.e. repeating information already entered into the data fields above). However, this field is meant to record more than a simple description; it is imperative that an attempt is made to clarify the reasons this deposit is being excavated at this time (i.e. stratigraphic relationships with surrounding contexts) and the reasons for any interpretation of the nature, function, or formation of the deposit (i.e. the specific data that supports an interpretation, as well as any data that does not). The NOTES field is also the place to discuss any differences in opinion between the excavator, the supervisor, the Field Director, and the Director of Excavations, and it is important to record the results of any dialogue that took place in the field or post-excavation relating to the deposit. It is not helpful or appropriate to treat this area as a personal diary; notes should be professional in tone as they will be archived for posterity and will appear unedited online (on ascsa.net).

For each deposit, the following information should be recorded:

1. Begin by stating what is being excavated and why it is being excavated at this time.
2. Include any descriptive information relating to the fields above that requires elaboration or clarification, including the relationship between this and other contexts.
3. Describe any contexts revealed by the excavation of this deposit (regardless of whether they will be excavated or not, e.g. bedrock): this will be of help during the composition of the Harris Matrix post-excavation. Note that context numbers may not have been assigned to these contexts yet, but they can still be described.
4. If there are expectations as to what will be revealed by the removal of this context, discuss them. Also discuss what is actually revealed, whether expected or unexpected.
5. Include any information about the excavation or revelation of this context that was not recorded in the data fields above.
6. Include any other information considered to be important regarding this deposit and how it relates to the greater excavation area.

6.3. CUTS

While deposits and structures are positive features, a cut is the remainder of a negative human action—the removal of something—and the interface between what was disturbed and what was later deposited or constructed atop this disturbance. Being negative, a cut cannot be excavated—only observed and described. To give a modern and extreme example, a cut would result if a family chose to build a swimming pool, dug the hole, and then changed their minds and backfilled it. Future archaeologists would need to record the cut of the swimming pool as documentation of that intended action. A more ancient example is the removal of a pithos and filling the subsequent cut with rubbish: it is only the shape of the cut that held the pithos that tells us it was once there. Most archaeological cuts, however, are more mundane. They normally represent the human action of digging a pit, foundation, robbing trench, or grave, and as anthropogenic actions they must be recorded. Such recording (done on the CUT SHEET) is especially useful for understanding sequences when there are multiple intersecting pits. All cuts must be recorded and assigned a context number so they can be integrated into the Harris Matrix, as they are part of the formation history of the site as a whole. Cuts can be distinguished in the field by a marking of the boundary between two deposits, and normally they are either curved or linear in shape. This boundary can be distinct, such as a clear difference in color or composition, or it can be subtle, such as a slight difference in compaction between the deposit filling the cut and the deposit disturbed by the cut. Cuts can only be recorded after they have been fully revealed (i.e. all deposits filling them have been excavated), except in certain situations when the cut is too deep to safely remove all fills and excavation must be halted arbitrarily.

6.3.1. Title Tag

See §6.2.1.

6.3.2. Coordinates

See §6.2.5.

6.3.3. Elevations

Several representative elevations should be taken along the top and bottom of the cut and recorded on the top plan of the cut (see §4.2). Of these, the highest value is entered in the TOP field and the lowest in the BOTTOM field.

6.3.4. Shape in Plan

Describe the shape at the top of the cut. Choose from the following terms:

SHAPE IN PLAN
Square
Rectangular
Circular
Semi-circular (a circular cut truncated by a later cut)
Oval
Sub-rectangular (roughly square or rectangular but with curved corners)
Linear
Irregular*

*If the term "Irregular" is used, the shape of the cut in plan must be described in greater detail in the Notes field (see §6.3.14).

6.3.5. Dimensons

If the shape of the cut is asymmetrical (i.e. not a circle or a square), measure the longest distance first. This is the **length,** while the shortest distance is the **width,** and the **depth** is the difference between the highest top elevation and the lowest bottom elevation. All measurements are recorded in meters. If the cut is square, the length and width will be the same measurement. If the cut is a circle, provide the **diameter** rather than the length and width.

6.3.6. Break of Slope –Top

Describe the degree at which the top surface of the edge of the cut breaks into the sides (Fig. 20a). Choose from the following terms:

BREAK IN SLOPE -TOP
Sharp   nearly 45 degrees to the top surface;
                         angular and regular in section

Gradual   rounded; gradually reaching close to 45
                         degrees or less

Imperceptible   no clear cut; more of a mild slope

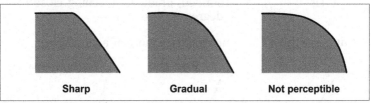

Figure 20a. Diagram for describing the slope at the top of a cut. Drawing
J. Herbst, after Spence 1994

6.3.7. Sides

Describe the sides of the cut using one of the following
terms:

SIDES:
Vertical
Convex
Concave
Stepped
Mixed*

*If the term "Mixed" is used, the appearance of the sides of the
cut must be described in greater detail in the NOTES field (see
§6.3.14).

6.3.8. Break of Slope – Base

Describe the degree at which the sides break into the base of the cut (Fig. 20b). Choose from the following terms:

BREAK OF SLOPE - BASE

Sharp   nearly 45 degrees to the top surface; angular and regular in section

Gradual   rounded; gradually reaching close to 45 degrees or less

Not perceptible   no clear cut; more of a mild slope

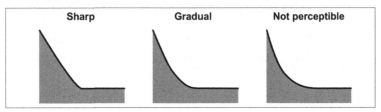

Figure 20b. Diagram for describing the slope at the base of a cut. Drawing J. Herbst, after Spence 1994

6.3.9. Base

Describe the base of the cut using one of the following terms (Fig. 20c):

BASE
Flat
Concave
Sloping (to the N, S, E, W, etc.)
Pointed
Tapered – blunt
Tapered – sharp
Uneven*

*If the term "Uneven" is used, the appearance of the base of the cut must be described in greater detail in the NOTES field.

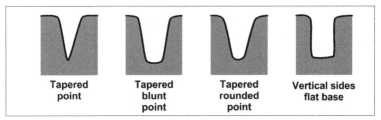

Figure 20c. Diagram for describing the base of a cut. Drawing J. Herbst, after Spence 1994

66

6.3.10. Orientation

The ORIENTATION field only applies to linear cuts. If linear, note the orientation of the cut in cardinal directions (N–S, E–W, NE–SW, NW–SE).

6.3.11. Truncation

Does the cut have its original shape, or has it been truncated (cut or disturbed) by another action/context? If the latter, use the TRUNCATION field to describe what part of the cut is truncated and, if possible, provide an interpretation of the later action that truncated the cut and any context numbers associated with the later action.

6.3.12. Harris Matrix

See §1.4 for an introduction to the principles of the Harris Matrix and §6.2.10 for instructions on using the Harris Matrix to record deposits. Using the Harris Matrix to record cuts is very similar. The principal difference between these two types of contexts is that the cut is included as an interface between deposits, structures, and other cuts. Note that cuts are expressed with ovals in the final Harris Matrix produced for the site as a whole.

6.3.13. Filled By

Use the FILLED BY field to list the context numbers of **all the deposits that filled this cut.**

6.3.14. Notes

For each cut, the following information should be recorded:

1. Include any descriptive information relating to the fields above that needs elaboration or clarification.
2. Describe how the cut was recognized.
3. Describe any contexts that this cut interrupts or is interrupted by: this will be of help during the composition of the Harris Matrix post-excavation. Note that

context numbers may not have been assigned to these contexts yet, but their physical relationships can be described.

4. Cuts of pits, trenches, and graves are important, as the material from the fill inside them and the deposits they cut can be very good dating tools. Describe how this cut and its related deposits might aid in the dating of this part of the site.

5. Include any information about this cut that was not recorded in the data fields above.

If any additions are made to the NOTES field post-excavation, they must be labeled "Later notes" and dated and initialed on the CUT SHEET and in the database.

6.4. STRUCTURES

Structures are purposely built features such as walls, built floors, built roadways, hearths, and wellheads. The STRUCTURE SHEET is designed to best record a built feature that is primarily composed of materials other than soil. Each moment of human action in regard to structures is recorded individually and assigned its own context number. For example, if a wall has a separately built foundation and superstructure, a threshold block that has been raised, and a door that has been later blocked up, each of these four separate actions will be assigned its own context number and STRUCTURE SHEET.

On the STRUCTURE SHEET and in the database, be sure to check the appropriate box to note whether or not the structure has been EXCAVATED (NO or YES).

6.4.1. Title Tag

See §6.2.1.

6.4.2. Chronological Range

If the structure being recorded has been excavated, the CHRONOLOGICAL RANGE field will take into account the same data as if it were a deposit (pottery, coins, or other [which can be a small find or stratigraphic relationship]; see §6.2.2). However, many walls and other structures at Corinth are left unexcavated according to government regulations or so that they may be preserved for public display. When this is the case, the structure can only be dated based on the chronological ranges of stratigraphically related contexts. Ideally, this would take the form of floors that are contemporary with the structure or material from the structure's foundation trench cut (see §3.4). However, if no foundation trenches exist for a structure, other stratigraphic relationships established in the field and recorded in the Harris Matrix must be used. For example: Does the structure cut any floors, pits, or other contexts, and thus post-date them (i.e. these contexts serve as a terminus post quem for the structure)? Are there any deposits or other structures that overlie the structure, and thus post-date it (i.e. these contexts serve as a terminus ante quem for the structure)?

This field is not filled out until the end of the season, when all available evidence can be assessed.

6.4.3. Coordinates

Based on the measurements of the size and shape of the structure, determine the furthest north, south, east, and west that the structure extends and record these values in the COORDINATES field. The top plan will be useful here.

6.4.4. Elevations

ELEVATIONS should be taken at several points on the structure, but only the highest and the lowest values are recorded in this field—record these in the TOP and BOTTOM fields, respectively. The other measurements should be added to the top plan.

6.4.5. Dimensions

Record the overall length, width, and height of the structure in meters and record these values in the DIMENSIONS field.

6.4.6. Materials

Use the MATERIALS field to list all forms of building material used in the structure. If there are different materials and they are being used in different and purposeful ways (for example, if marble is used only on the corners, or large stones only at the base of a wall), then elaborate here and discuss again in the NOTES field (see §6.4.19).

Frequently used building materials at Corinth include limestone, sandstone, marble, andesite, conglomerate roof tiles, diamond tiles, brick (fired), mud brick, clay plaster, hydroplaster, cement, stone tesserae, and glass tesserae.

6.4.7. Size of Materials

Measure several examples of each type of building material in the structure, and list the average size for each type (in meters) in the SIZE OF MATERIALS field.

6.4.8. Finish of Stones

The FINISH OF STONES field describes the exterior surface of any stones used in the structure (see Fig. 21 below). It should not be applied to other forms of building material; if no stones used are used in the structure, leave this field blank. Choose from the following terms:

FINISH OF STONES

Unworked	essentially raw field stones
Roughly hewn	field stones roughly worked so that they have roughly regular, angular surfaces
Squared	similar to roughly hewn but more elaborate and angular
Mixed	mixed finish; also noting whether the surface is Tooled or Smoothed/Polished

If the surface of the stones is tooled, describe the appearance of the tool marks in the NOTES field (see §6.4.19). If the structure is described as "Mixed," a full description of the different finishes of stones must be included in the NOTES field. Often, a change observed in the masonry style or the building materials used in a structure is evidence of a later repair or addition to the structure and therefore a new phase of the structure's use. Make sure that this is not the case here: all repairs and additions to a structure must be recorded separately and assigned their own context number.

If a wall is being recorded and the two faces are significantly different from one another, select the "Mixed" option and then describe each face in the NOTES field, explaining the differences observed.

6.4.9. Masonry Style

The MASONRY STYLE field is only applicable to structures built up from the ground (not, for example, built roads, built floors, built hearths, mosaics, etc.). First, provide a general description of the way the structure was built. Only if possible, be more specific to the Classical world and to Corinth. In this field, select from the following general terms:

MASONRY STYLE	
Dumped rubble	present in some foundations
Uncoursed	no regular coures or regular horizontal alignment
Random courses	courses of varied and random height
Regular courses	courses of regular and consistent height
Coursed	
Mixed	

Also state whether any of the following techniques are used in conjunction with the masonry style:

MASONRY TECHNIQUES

String Course	a projecting course of tile, brick, or stone to emphasize a junction or boundary
Leveling Course	a course of building material used to create a level surface upon which to continue building upwards
Quoins	stressed corners
Revetment	wall surfaces usually faced with marble or other fine stone slabs

Next, only if possible use the masonry terms in Fig. 21, which are specific to the Classical world.

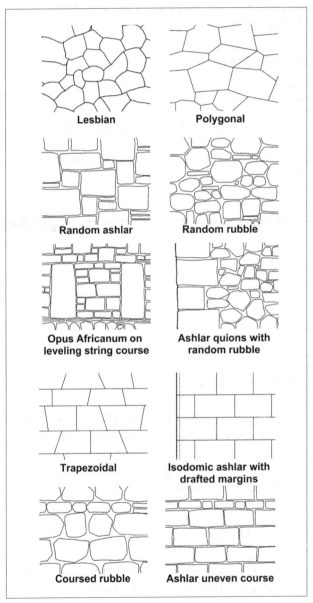

Figure 21. Diagram of stone finishes and masonry styles.
Drawing J. Herbst, after Spence 1994

6.4.10. Bonding Material

Describe the BONDING MATERIAL of the structure. Choose one of the following terms:

BONDING MATERIAL
None
Mud-plaster
Plaster
Cement
Modern cement (from modern restoration work)

If clamps are present (Fig. 22), it is also important to record them in the BONDING MATERIAL field.

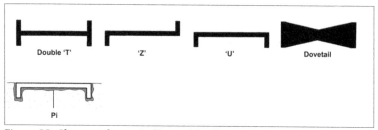

Figure 22. Clamp styles typically used in Classical Antiquity. Drawing J. Herbst

6.4.11. Special Features

List any significant special features of this structure, such as: masons' marks, spolia, graffiti, or evidence for tools or quarrying methods used on stones (e.g. Lewis holes and surface treatments), arches or vaults, thresholds or windows, etc. This field is only used to list the special features—describe the features fully in the NOTES field (see §6.4.19).

6.4.12. Harris Matrix

See §1.4 for an introduction to the principles of the Harris Matrix and §6.2.10 for instructions on using the Harris Matrix to record deposits. Using the Harris Matrix to record structures is very similar; the principal difference is that there is no comparison between structures and their surrounding contexts, as structures are easily distinguished from the surrounding soil. Note that structures are expressed as rectangles in the final Harris Matrix produced for the site as a whole.

6.4.13. Formation/Interpretation

In the FORMATION/INTERPRETATION field, provide a brief interpretation of the nature and function of the structure. The NOTES field (see §6.4.19) should include a discussion of the evidence for this interpretation. This field will be useful in creating the TITLE TAG for this context. Choose from the following terms:

FORMATION/INTERPRETATION
Wall-superstructure or Wall-foundation wall
Repair/addition
Built floor
Built road or metaled road (constructed with gravel or crushed stone)
Built hearth
Wellhead
Drain manhole
Stairs
Platform (or stylobate)
Ramp
Pier

6.4.14. Internal or External Structure

This field will only be used if the structure being recorded is a wall. In this instance, provide an interpretation as to whether it is an external or an internal wall—or whether one face is internal and the other external—and provide evidence to support the interpretation (including, if necessary, any related structures or other contexts that support the interpretation). If this is not possible with the evidence available, explain why.

6.4.15. Related Contexts

In the RELATED CONTEXTS field, briefly mention any and all directly related structures along with their context numbers. Define the relationship: Do they bond or not?

Are they physically connected or related by stratigraphy or building style?

Also briefly discuss the structure being recorded in the context of the greater building activities of this moment: Is it part of a room, a building, or a city block? Is it part of a campaign of later refurbishment, remodeling, or repair?

Lastly, mention all physically related deposits and cuts: floors, foundation or robbing trenches, and their cuts—anything directly associated with the structure being recorded. This field is used to list all related contexts; use the NOTES field (see §6.4.19) to more fully describe these relationships.

6.4.16. Dry Sieving

The DRY SIEVING field will only be used if the structure being recorded is subsequently excavated/dismantled. If so, treat all soil inside the structure as if it were a deposit. All material culture found in the structure will be given the same context number as the wall, and it should be noted on the STRUCTURE SHEET and in the database that this wall was excavated.

Indicate whether or not this deposit was dry-sieved (see §2.5), the size of the mesh sieve that was used (at Corinth we typically use 5 mm), and the percent of the total context that was sieved. The latter can be estimated by counting the number of buckets or wheelbarrows of soil that are removed during excavation and then calculating the ratio between those taken to the dump and those taken to be sieved. Soil from inside structures is always 100 percent dry sieved unless it is deemed necessary to take a sample for flotation before the remainder is dry sieved.

6.4.17. Coins

See §6.2.16.

6.4.18. Finds Collected

See §6.2.17.

6.4.19. Notes

The NOTES field provides an opportunity to give an account in narrative form of any observations made about the structure being recorded and any interpretations or questions raised about the context or other aspects of the excavation in general. It is perfectly acceptable to be repetitive here if it is necessary to emphasize salient points (i.e. repeating information already entered into the data fields above). The NOTES field is also the place to discuss any differences in opinion between the excavator, the supervisor, the Field Director, and the Director of Excavations, and it is important to record the results of any dialogue that took place in the field or post-excavation relating to the structure. It is not helpful or appropriate to treat this area as a personal diary; notes should be professional in tone as they will be archived for posterity and will appear unedited online (on ascsa.net).

For each structure, the following information should be recorded:

1. Describe specific evidence supporting or contradicting the interpretation of the nature and function of this structure.
2. Provide an analysis of the relationship between this structure and other structures in the excavation area.
3. Provide any descriptive information relating to the fields above that requires elaboration or clarification.
4. State whether this structure is to be excavated or will be left for presentation on site, as well as the reason for this choice.
5. List any letters, numbers, or other names assigned to this structure in previous excavations (these can be found by examining previous excavation records in consultation with the Director of Excavations).

7. BURIALS AND SKELETONS

Recording burials requires documenting each action that went into burying the individual(s) present in the grave. For example, the digging of a grave leaves a grave cut; next, a sarcophagus may be placed in the grave (or if the body was cremated, it may have been placed in an ossuary before burial); the body may be placed in the grave; and possibly later the grave may be reopened and the bones of the skeleton and/or grave goods manipulated as part of a secondary burial ritual. Each of these actions is an individual context that requires individual recording so that it can be incorporated into the Harris Matrix of the site and thereby contribute to a more nuanced understanding of mortuary activity. Grave cuts, grave fills, and sarcophagi should be recorded with CUT, DEPOSIT, and STRUCTURE SHEETS, respectively. Skeletons, whether articulated or disarticulated, are recorded with a SKELETON SHEET.

In certain complicated situations, such as when a female skeleton is buried with a fetus in position or in the case of a mass grave, there might be multiple discernable individual skeletons in the same context. Each individual articulated skeleton must be recorded separately. Disarticulated bones may have originally belonged to more than one individual, but at the time of excavation they are discovered as part of the same moment in time and should be recorded with the same context number.

Make sure to take soil samples for flotation from the fill of the grave (see §7.12)

If necessary, BONE LOT NUMBERS will be assigned at the end of the season and/or by the anthropologist studying the remains.

7.1. COORDINATES, ELEVATIONS, AND ORIENTATION

The COORDINATES should reflect the northern, southern, eastern, and western extents of the skeleton. Use these fields to determine the MAX DIMENSIONS (LENGTH, WIDTH, and DEPTH) of the skeleton. ELEVATIONS should be taken at various points on the skeleton before and after removal (these should be recorded on the top plan), but only the elevations taken on top of the skull (TOP OF SKULL) and on the earth after the skull is removed (BOTTOM OF SKULL) should be recorded in this field. Using a compass, take a bearing from pelvis to skull; record the BEARING and draw a NORTH ARROW in the box provided in the skeleton diagram below (see §7.6).

7.2. TYPE

The TYPE field asks for a simple description of the type of burial being recorded. As with the TITLE TAG (see §6.2.1), this description should be very brief. Examples of sufficient descriptions include:

TYPE
Cist/pit
Pit lined with tiles
Cremation in urn
Rock-cut tomb with multiple burials
Bone stack
Inhumation in sarcophagus

7.3. GRAVE CUT AND FILL(S)

The GRAVE CUT and FILL(S) fields ask for the context numbers of the grave cut and all fills inside the cut. These fields are used only to list context numbers—not to describe the contexts—as they will have been described already on their own context recording sheets.

7.4. SARCOPHAGUS/OSSUARY

Only enter information in the SARCOPHAGUS/OSSUARY field if the skeleton was buried in a sarcophagus or some other kind of ossuary, such as a ceramic vessel or a coffin. If the burial was in a sarcophagus or other stone-built container, this should be recorded with a STRUCTURE SHEET, then the context number entered here. If there was some other kind of ossuary, such as a ceramic vessel or a roof tile, this item should be recorded as a small find and may be inventoried in the museum. If the item receives a museum inventory number, enter the number in this field. If the burial contained either a sarcophagus or an ossuary, circle this term in the field name on the SKELETON SHEET.

Wooden coffins were used at different periods at Corinth, but the wood rarely survives. Often, however, the presence of a coffin can be reconstructed by making careful note of where the coffin nails are found around the skeleton. Coffins (even if they survive only as nails) should be given a context number, incorporated into the Harris Matrix, and recorded on a DEPOSIT SHEET.

7.5. TRUNCATION AND
LATER DISTURBANCES/TRUNCATION

The principle of "Last In, First Out" means that when an individual skeleton is recorded, any later truncations or disturbances should have already been recorded and/or removed as individual contexts. The term **disturbance** describes later action that is burial-related, such as if the skeleton was disturbed by the deposition of a second burial in the same grave. But truncation is later action that is not related to the burial activities of this particular grave(s) and cuts or that removes part of the burial contexts, such as a later wall being founded over part of the grave, or a later unrelated burial cutting through the skeleton. If the skeleton has been truncated by later action, list the context number(s) of these actions in the TRUNCATION field. Use the larger field below, LATER DISTURBANCES/TRUNCATION, to briefly describe any instances of truncation or disturbance. Any natural action from roots or animals should also be described in this field. If this space is not sufficient, continue the description in the EXCAVATION NOTES field (see §7.14).

7.6. SKELETON DIAGRAM

In the skeleton diagram, shade in the bones that are present at the time of excavation. Use a hashed line to show any truncation. Draw the NORTH ARROW and note the compass BEARING (taken from pelvis to skull) in the box provided. Use the checkboxes to note whether the skeleton is ARTICULATED or DISARTICULATED and a PRIMARY or SECONDARY burial.

7.7. STICK-FIGURE SKETCH

In the STICK-FIGURE SKETCH field, draw a crude sketch of the body as it lies in the grave, expressing the position of the head and limbs in particular. This field is simply a thumbnail of the larger, more detailed top plan. Do not sketch secondary burials, such as bone piles, here—the top plan and photographs will be sufficient for these types of burials.

7.8. HARRIS MATRIX

See §1.4 for an introduction to the principles of the Harris Matrix and §6.2.10 for instructions on using the Harris Matrix to record deposits. As with other contexts, a skeleton will form a distinct unit in the Harris Matrix. The cut and deposit(s) and their relationships to other contexts should be expressed in the same way as any other excavated context.

7.9. GENERAL POSITION OF BODY

The GENERAL POSITION OF BODY field and the related fields below it should only be completed for articulated skeletons, not bone piles. Describe the position of the body and its different parts in the appropriate fields. In the GENERAL

POSITION OF BODY field, note whether the skeleton is prone (face down), supine (face up), extended or flexed, and laying on the left or the right side. Note which way the HEAD faces and if it is propped by stones or other materials. If the body is twisted or half supine or half on its side, note this in the TRUNK field. In the RIGHT ARM & HAND and LEFT ARM & HAND fields, note whether the arms are straight or flexed, at the side, crossed over the chest, on the pelvis, or under the body, and describe the position of the hands (open or clenched, palms up or down, fingers entwined or grasping an object, etc.). In the RIGHT LEG & FOOT and LEFT LEG & FOOT fields, note whether the legs are extended or flexed, side-by-side, or crossed (left over right or right over left), and describe the position of the feet (pointing down or up, splayed to either side, etc.).

7.10. LIST IN SITU BROKEN BONES

List any bones that were broken before excavation began. Use the checkboxes to note if the state of preservation of the bones is GOOD, FAIR, or POOR. Use Figs. 23 and 24 to identify the bones of an adult, a sub-adult, or a neonate.

7.11. ASSOCIATED OBJECTS

In the ASSOCIATED OBJECTS field, note the items directly associated with the skeleton, including the remains of any clothing and accessories on the skeleton or any grave goods deliberately placed in the grave at the time of burial. Do not list every type of material that happens to be in the fill of the grave cut, as much of it will be unintentional. If any of these items are inventoried in the museum, add the museum inventory numbers to this field on the SKELETON SHEET.

7.12. DRY SIEVING AND FLOTATION SAMPLES

Consult with the Director of Excavations and the Field Director before removing the skeleton. It might be fruitful to take several soil samples for flotation (see §2.6) at

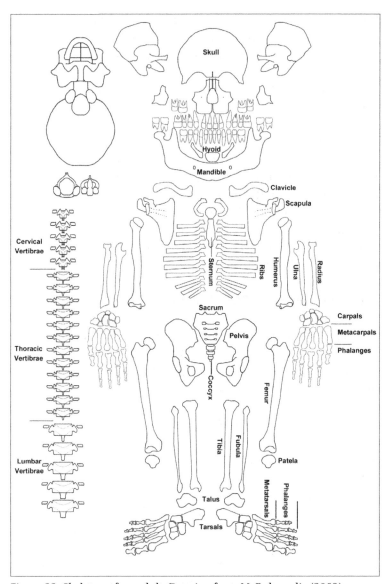

Figure 23. Skeleton of an adult. Drawing from M. Roksandic (2003)

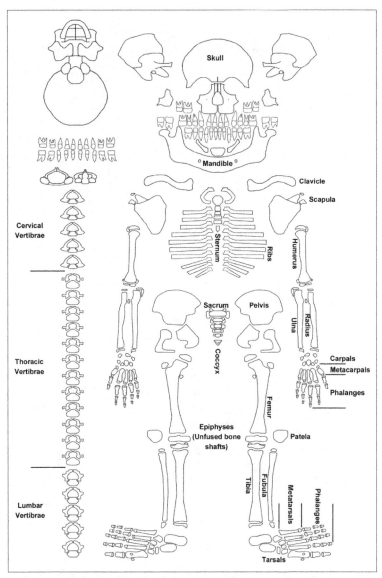

Figure 24a. Skeleton of a sub-adult. Drawing from M. Roksandic (2003)

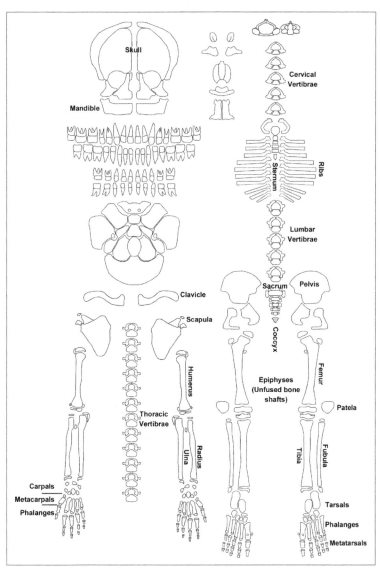

Figure 24b. Skeleton of a neonate. Drawing from M. Roksandic (2003)

different points on top of, beside, and under the body to determine whether the remains of perishable grave goods can be detected in the soil and to identify where they were placed on or around the body. A SAMPLE SHEET must be filled out for each water floatation sample (see §2.6.1). Whatever soil is not sampled should be 100 percent dry sieved with a fine mesh. It is the responsibility of every team member to ensure that the sieving action is not so harsh that it damages any bone still in the loose soil.

7.13. SPECIALIST OSTEOLOGICAL DATA

The fields in this section will be completed by an osteologist post-excavation.

7.14. EXCAVATION NOTES

Use the EXCAVATION NOTES field to more fully describe the state of the skeleton and the way it was buried, any disturbances or truncation, the way the skeleton or the sarcophagus/ossuary is situated within the grave cut, or any physical remains of burial ritual or practice. Describe in detail any complicated burial situations, such as a female with fetus in position or multiple burials in the same cut or multiple cuts.

7.15. DRAWINGS

The site architect will produce a professional plan of each burial, but each skeleton also needs a measured top plan (see §4.1 and 4.2). As skeletons are more difficult to draw, consider using a drawing frame if it can be used without damaging the skeleton—consult the architect or the Field Director for advice, if necessary. Include the grave cut in the drawing of the skeleton, as well as the position of clothing, accessories, and grave goods.

8. FINDS

8.1. FINDS LABELS IN THE FIELD

Wooden tags are available for labeling the buckets and boxes used to collect pottery and tile excavated from each context. According to the Corinth Excavations system, each supervisor or supervisory pair is assigned a different color tag to help them distinguish their own contexts. The following information should be written in pencil on the tag: the **area of excavation** (e.g. TESE), the **context number**, and the **date**.

Other finds (such as bone/shell, coins, glass, metal objects, etc.) are collected separately by type in envelopes (or boxes, if necessary) and taken to the museum for specialized cleaning, analysis, and recording—with the exception of bone, which is taken with the pottery for processing. The following information should be written on the envelope or box: the **type of material** or find collected, the **context number**, the **date**, and the **team color**.

8.2. POTTERY

Pottery is the most prolific type of find on site, and almost every deposit and excavated structure will yield pottery. Large amounts of pottery are collected in a basket or bucket, while small amounts are collected in a box. All pottery is taken to the pot sheds to be washed and laid out to dry; the foreman is responsible for this task. Pottery can remain on site overnight if the entire context from which it was collected is not yet fully washed, or if the context is still being excavated. While in the field, note on the appropriate context recording sheet the number of baskets and boxes of pottery that were collected, as this information will be helpful during pottery reading.

8.3. UNWORKED ANIMAL BONE AND SHELL

Unworked animal bone and shell from any given context are collected together in the same box and properly labeled. The bone/shell from this context will be taken to the pot sheds along with the pottery; the foreman is responsible for this task. A basic reading of the bone and shell is made by the Director of Excavations while he/she identifies the pottery. Any special features should be noted and the bone should be weighed. Significant contexts of bone and shell, which may be interpreted as coming from a kitchen or other special-use area that can be chronologically dated, may be saved as a "lot" for future examination by a faunal specialist.

8.4. ROOF TILES

Small fragments of roof tile are a frequent find in deposits at Corinth and are of little value in dating the context. Whole tiles or tiles with a preserved edge or that show the shape of the tile are more informative. For this reason, a fall of roof tiles or a deposit of dumped destruction debris in a pit, well, or cistern should be treated more carefully. Collect the tiles in the field, weigh them, note whether they are Laconian (round in profile) or Corinthian (flat in profile; see §12.4.1), describe them (e.g. if they are pan or cover tiles, painted or plain), and estimate the percentage of each by weight in the NOTES field on the DEPOSIT SHEET or STRUCTURE SHEET. Lay out any broken tile fragments from destruction debris and look for joins. If no joins can be made between many broken tile fragments, this suggests that the context is not a primary deposit of destruction debris. If a complete profile can be reconstructed, sketch the tile and describe its dimensions (length, width, thickness, and height). All whole tiles should be taken to the pot sheds along with the pottery from the same context. Non-descript, non-joining tiles should be left on site.

8.5. COINS

For more information on coins, see §6.2.16. Coins are taken to the museum and registered with the Assistant Director of Excavations or the conservator after work ends each day. Each coin is assigned a sequential and unique number to aid in future study. Coins are cleaned by the conservator and analyzed by the numismatist; their identifications are returned later for recording on the applicable context recording sheets and in the database by the supervisor.

8.6. "SMALL FINDS"

As described in §8.1, small finds are any man-made items recovered from the excavation that are not pottery, unworked animal bone/shell, roof tiles, or coins. In most cases, small finds will be glass or small objects made of metal or worked bone, and they will be part of a fill (i.e. not in primary deposition). Each type of find should be collected together in a separate box or envelope (metals collected together, glass collected together, etc.) and the boxes and envelopes labeled with the area of excavation, date, context number from which the material came, and type of material. In-situ finds (see below) should be treated more method-ically: they must be recorded individually (typically with their own context number), sketched, and photographed. **All small finds must be brought to the museum at the end of the day;** they cannot remain on site, even if they come from a context that is still being excavated at the end of the day. Wall plaster should be collected separately and sent to the pot sheds for counting and weighing.

8.7. OBJECTS FOUND IN SITU

In-situ objects require special procedures and should be excavated with extra care in order to preserve their spatial relationships at the time of excavation. The conservator should be consulted during excavation and he/she may decide to consolidate and excavate the finds personally. In-situ objects resting on interfaces such as floors and surfaces or the cut of a pit are the result of a discrete human action. Their deposition reflects a moment in time that is separate from the creation of the interface upon which they rest and the fill that covers them. Each of these assemblages must be assigned its own context number (different from the fill that covers them), drawn and photographed, and collected separately. For example, a group of metal tools resting on a floor surface is best understood as a depositional act in and of itself, rather than simply a find related to whatever fill that covered it or the floor upon which it rested. In the case of multiple objects found together, such as several whole vessels found in a foundation deposit, these objects may receive the same context number, but should be given temporary alphabetic field markers to aid in later identification (e.g. 5801-A, 5801-B, etc.). Coordinate measurements, as well as top and bottom elevations, should be taken on each object. Later, many (if not all) of the objects will receive museum inventory numbers. These numbers should be recorded on the appropriate context recording sheets and communicated back to the conservator, Field Director, supervisor, and architect so their records can be updated.

9. GUIDELINES FOR EXCAVATION SUMMARIES

Supervisors collaborate with the Field Director to create a summary of the findings of the excavation in their assigned areas. At the end of the excavation, these reports are used to write an end of season report. Most of the supervisors will work as a team to summarize the open-area excavation as a whole, while others might be recording the excavation of the contexts associated with a single room or other feature; in this case, these parts of the excavation will be written up separately. New summaries that build upon the summaries of the previous excavation season need only to be updated as necessary. Summaries are organized chronologically from earliest to latest, and they are meant to provide an overall impression of the excavation (i.e. the "high points")—not a regurgitation of every context that was recorded (e.g. soil descriptions should not appear in a summary report unless they are an important characteristic of a layer). Example summaries from past seasons are available on ascsa.net for consultation. It is the responsibility of the Field Director to ensure that summaries are composed and to request corrections if needed. Both the Field Director and the Assistant Director will read the summaries and assess their content for clarity of expression, accuracy of the data discussed, and the synthesis that is produced. These documents will be uploaded to the database and ascsa.net and become a part of the permanent archive of the Excavations.

All summaries must be accompanied by an up-to-date Harris Matrix that is annotated with chronological markers and any other useful information as needed (see §1.4 and §6.2.10). This document also will be checked by the Field Director and the Assistant Director.

9.1. GOALS OF THE SUMMARY

Supervisors are expected to submit to the Field Director and the Assistant Director both an "Interim Summary" at the midpoint of the excavation session and a "Final Summary" at the end. The use of the term "Summary" in the title is conventional and perhaps slightly misleading, as this document should resemble an excavation report of the kind published in *Hesperia* rather than a summary of the excavation activities. Summaries are preparatory documents for the publication of each year's campaign. Writing the summary requires shifting gears from the type of descriptive and interpretative writing appropriate to the NOTES field (located on the context recording sheets) in order to present a narrative of past events or activities that took place in the area supervised. Supervisors's thinking should expand from the scale of individual contexts to the scale of whole periods. The evidence for claims about past events should be taken from the contexts, such that the summary presents a narrative based on stratigraphy rather than a description of the stratigraphy itself.

9.2. ORGANIZATION/STRUCTURE

The stratigraphic sequence and the relationships of the contexts to each other will dictate the organization of the summary, as the overall structure of the document is chronological in nature. Discussion of the excavated area begins with the earliest datable activities (which are dated on the basis of the contexts) and moves through the most recent events. Although dates for the individual contexts are assigned on the basis of the pottery contained therein (and possibly on other identifiable material culture, such as coins), these dates may not correspond with those suggested by the stratigraphic sequence. The Harris Matrix will allow supervisors to adjust context dates on the basis of stratigraphic relationships.

9.3. FORMAL FEATURES

The summary should be typed. The header should contain the name(s) of the Director of Excavations, the Field Director, and the supervisors; the area excavated (e.g. Temple E, Southeast Excavations); and grid coordinates. The dates of excavation should go in the top left corner of the first page, but not in the header. A brief introduction includes the coordinates of the excavation area and where it is situated in relation to other excavated areas or large site features (e.g. Northwest passage, Balk N of Unit 2, Room G). The members of the excavation team and the positions they held also are listed, including the names of the supervisors, workmen (first and last), and staff. The dates during which excavations took place and the overall goals of the excavation season as they are known to the supervisors also are included.

The activities of each period are described in separate sections, each with an appropriate section heading (e.g. Late Roman, Byzantine). The summary should not be a list describing every single context recorded, but rather a description of significant features and phases and how they relate, so as to infer the processes that created them. For significant features, concrete information—including dimensions and northing and easting coordinates—should be included in order to locate them in space. Walls, pits, graves, hearths, and floors are examples of significant features. The summary is meant to describe past human activities that took place in the area, and as such these features should be tied to events or activities.

Significant coins and inventoried objects (along with their inventory numbers) are included in the summary to assist in the argumentation. They can be used as evidence for dating features and events, but also for arguing about functions and uses of space.

The conclusion should include a brief assessment of how the excavation has contributed to the questions set out at the beginning of work and any information that would assist further excavation in the area, such as any problems, unexcavated (or partially excavated) contexts, and any other information that may be important to note. A section should be included to highlight questions that remain unanswered by excavations so far.

9.4. DELIVERABLES

The "Interim Summary" should be written at the midpoint of the session, and the "Final Summary" will be uploaded to the database and ascsa.net at the end of the fourth week. The "Interim Summary" is an important exercise for working through the analysis of the excavated area and for obtaining feedback about the work, without the looming pressure of other end-of-session tasks. On other excavations, supervisors are rarely asked to attempt this level of synthesis, so this is a rare and exciting opportunity offered at Corinth Excavations. The summaries are a collaborative process and frequently require several rounds of revisions, suggestions, and discussion with the Field Director and the Assistant Director.

9.5. TIPS FOR WRITING THE SUMMARY

The summary is a synthesis and not simply a facsimile of the context recording sheets. Descriptions of particular contexts—unless pertinent or used as evidence for interpretative claims—should be avoided because this information is recorded elsewhere and is easily available on the context recording sheets. For example, it would be useful to note that a building went out of use during a certain period because a particular fill covered over the top of a wall. In this case, the following statement would be acceptable: "And then the courtyard was expanded, and a single unified surface was constructed over it (context X) and the room to the south, uniting the two spaces and suggesting that they were being used in the same ways." This statement should not read:

"And then we had to start excavating in the room south of the courtyard since the stratigraphy overlapped with the courtyard." It is nearly impossible to compose this level of interpretative narrative without a final, phased and annotated Harris Matrix. Nevertheless, the process of composing the "Interim Summary" must be started with the first few contexts excavated. Claims may always be adjusted later as understanding of the area and the processes shaping it develops. Examples of previous summaries are used to guide supervisors in the thinking process necessary for composing their own summary.

10. POTTERY READING

10.1. SORTING

Every afternoon, each supervisor is responsible for sorting the pottery from the contexts they recorded in the field. Supervisors are encouraged to assist in the sorting of all pottery once it is washed—even from contexts recorded by other supervisors—so that a backlog does not develop as the excavation progresses. Instruction is given on pottery types and sorting procedures at the beginning of each excavation session.

First, the decorated/fine wares are separated from the coarse wares and cooking wares, and then any diagnostic sherds (rims, bases, handles, and decorated sherds) from each category are set apart. Any other objects that look unusual should be set apart and shown to the Director of Excavations during the reading. Any bones, metal, or glass items that were missed in the field and brought to the pot sheds—as well as any tiles and rocks—should be placed at the top of the table.

10.2. READING

The Director of Excavations is responsible for reading the pottery, and he/she will dictate what information is recorded in the database for each context, as well as assign a date to the pottery. As far as possible, standardized terms for vessel forms are used to identify pottery, but inventory numbers and published references may also be used.

10.3. POTTERY DATABASE FIELDS

The database versions of the DEPOSIT SHEETS and STRUCTURE SHEETS contain pottery fields for the recording of pottery during the pottery reading. Since the pottery from many contexts is eventually discarded or partially discarded, these records are an essential part of the excavation archive. The Director of Excavations will determine what information is entered into these fields, and it is the responsibility of the supervisor who recorded the context in the field to record the pottery at the reading. In the database under the POTTERY tab, the pottery date should be recorded, along with whether the pottery has been "saved," "partially saved," or "thrown." At the end of the reading of each context, the Director of Excavations must decide whether to save or throw the pottery. This decision is based on the material itself and on the stratigraphic relationships between this context and the rest of the site.

10.4. SAVED AND THROWN POTTERY

Saved pottery is counted and weighed and set aside for later consultation. This pottery must be placed in a box or tin with a wooden label marked "Saved." **A note may be made as to why the pottery is being saved (ask the Director of Excavations for input):** Is it being saved for mending, for lotting, or to see how the stratigraphy develops as more of the site is excavated? "Saved" status is noted in the database and on the wooden tag. Pottery can also be "partially saved," wherein the rest of the context is "thrown."

Pottery is "thrown" when the Director of Excavations has retrieved all the useful information from a given context, and it is of no further use. The sheer volume of pottery collected during each excavation season makes it impossible to indefinitely save and store all pottery. "Thrown" status must also be noted in the database and on the wooden tag. After weighing and counting "thrown" pottery, place it in a tin on the shelves in the pot sheds; it will be reburied later.

"Saved," "thrown," or "partially saved" should be typed into the database below the WEIGHTS and COUNTS fields, and any additional notes should be typed there. If a context is "partially saved," the HELD box next to READ POTTERY TO BE SAVED should be checked.

10.5. POTTERY WEIGHTS AND COUNTS

Enter the counts and weights of sherds by category (coarse, semi-coarse, fine, and cooking) for the entire context in the ORIGINAL column. If pottery is wholly or partially "Saved," the saved pieces must be counted and weighed separately— enter these counts and weights in the FINAL column. Again, if a context is "partially saved," the HELD box must be checked.

10.6. "GOOD THINGS FROM BAD PLACES" (GTs)

This is a special category reserved for particularly interesting finds that were not found in their primary context; that is, they have been disturbed since their original deposition in the ground and are chance finds in another, often much later, context. GTs usually do not provide much information about the context in which they were found, but there may be a compelling reason to save them anyway. GTs are weighed and counted with the rest of the context, and this information is entered in the ORIGINAL column. Normally, if a GT is saved, the rest of the context is thrown, so the GT is the FINAL WEIGHT; this should be indicated in the SAVED/THROWN free-text field (e.g. "thrown, with one GT"). GTs must be brought to the museum after pottery reading, where they are labeled with their context number and placed in a box for lotting (see §11). Check the GT box next to this item in the database.

11. LOTTING

In conceptual terms, a **lot** is a group of individual contexts that can be meaningfully grouped together as an archaeologically understandable feature, such as a pit, a floor, or a foundation trench. In practical terms, a lot represents the finds from these feature that decide their date and represent the type of material within them. Material that becomes a lot is saved and permanently stored. This process takes place at the end of the excavation season.

The actual process of lotting involves creating a careful record of which contexts have been saved and which contexts have been thrown during each pottery session, both in the database and on the context recording sheets. The next step is to organize the contexts with saved pottery into meaningful stratigraphic and historical events, such as the contexts that make up the fill of a pit, a floor level, or a foundation trench. The composition of an annotated Harris Matrix is therefore very helpful during the lotting process.

Lots are numbered by year, so the first lot would be Lot 2017-001. The Field Director composes the final lot list, with brief descriptions of each lot along with its context numbers, and then enters the lots into the database. A paper list of the lot numbers, brief lot descriptions, and the contexts included is printed and stored in the museum.

The lotting process is also a good time to determine mending and conserving priorities.

Example 1:
Context 76 is the floor associated with the N–S wall
Context 78 is the fill of the foundation trench for the N–S wall covered by a floor (76)

In terms of lotting, although these two contexts are related by their association with the same building, they should be kept separate as two different phases of the history of the building (i.e. the construction and the use), and therefore also as two different lots (e.g. Lots 2017-001 and 2017-002).

Example 2:
Context 48 is destruction debris consisting mostly of tile
Context 50 is destruction debris consisting primarily of mudbrick; 50 is beneath 48
Context 52 is the clay floor beneath 50

Contexts 48 and 50 likely can be understood as two contexts created by the same destruction event and so as part of the same phase of the history of this building; these will be stored as a single lot (Lot 2017-003). They are lotted separately from the floor (Context 52; Lot 2017-004), as this context is not part of the phase of destruction, but rather of the use phase of the building.

Once saved and partially-saved contexts have been sorted into potential lots, they should be discussed with the Field Director and the Director of Excavations. At this point, the Director of Excavations will make the final decision as to what pottery will be lotted, and the Field Director will assign lot numbers. All pottery within a single lot is then labeled with the lot number and placed on the storage shelves in the pot sheds. Note that although multiple contexts may be assigned to the same lot, the **pottery from different contexts is never physically combined**, but rather stored separately. Any small finds that belong with lotted contexts that are completely saved are stored with the pottery.

When lot numbers are assigned, they must be added to the necessary database entries and the context recording sheets. Previously saved and partially-saved pottery that was not assigned to a lot should be marked as "thrown" in the database and on the context recording sheets. For pottery that was lotted, the ALL HELD button should be clicked in the database so that the HELD boxes are checked beside each pottery entry. In the field below WEIGHTS and COUNTS, the lot number should be recorded.

12. INVENTORYING IN THE MUSEUM

Corinth Excavations standardized the process of describing or "inventorying" objects that will be kept in the museum. The following section is a step-by-step description of that process and is intended to cover all types of material culture that might be chosen for inventorying by the Director of Excavations or the Assistant Director. Such objects tend to be unique examples of specific types of pottery or small finds or anything that has an inscription or graffito on it. Each object is numbered according to the type of material, the year of excavation, and then consecutively within that year.

Description of archaeological artifacts entails "the difficult job of finding appropriate words. In effect, writing a visual description consists of two separate acts of translation. The first transforms a visual experience into a verbal one and the second turns a private experience into one that can be communicated to someone else" (Munsterberg 2008–2009; thanks to Kathleen Slane for the reference). In order to achieve this end result, the generations of archaeologists who have catalogued artifacts in the collections of Corinth Excavations have compiled instructions and terminology that is used by supervisors duringthe post-excavation processing of the artifacts they find The collections are very rich, encompassing over 100,000 artifacts and 90,000 coins. A small percentage of these objects is described in the online catalogue entries at ascsa.net. A search for parallels in the collections is a very useful exercise for becoming familiar with the appropriate terminology for each class of artifact. It is important that descriptions of objects are both concise and accurate.

12.1. POTTERY

12.1.1. Numbering Artifacts

The number assigned to the object being inventoried involves four elements:

<u>Numbering Artifacts</u>

Type	the identifying letter from a pull-down menu: C for Pottery, MF for Miscellaneous Finds, L for Lamp
Year	the year of excavation
Number	a continuous number (leading zeros should not be used)
Suffix	a suffix (A, B, C, etc.) to distinguish non-joining parts of a single object

Examples: C 2004 1, C 2004 2A, C 2004 2B, C 2004 2C.

When inventorying several non-joining fragments of the same vase, complete a form with a full description of fragment A, incorporating information about vessel shape and decoration from all the pieces. For the rest of the fragments, refer to fragment A in the fields that are not specific to each fragment, and provide specific information such as condition, weight, and dimensions for each specific fragment.

When inventorying objects from the early excavations that have continuous numbers rather than years, leave the YEAR field blank (e.g. MF 13448).

12.1.2. Condition

CONDITION is the state of preservation of the object. Select one of the following options from the pull-down menu:

CONDITION

Complete or intact	unbroken or broken, but mended completely
Fragment	much or most is missing
Missing parts	most exists but is missing a small part (e.g. a statue missing its head). This option is best for statues and figurines.
Complete profile	all elements of the profile from foot to lip exist (handles and spouts are not necessary)

In addition to the pull-down menu, there is also a free-text field to describe object preservation. In addition to a general description of the fragment, describe the condition of the surface, glaze, slip, etc. When inventorying pottery, begin from the bottom of the vessel and move up. References to non-joining fragments left in lots can be included here.

Examples:
Four joining frgts preserve all of foot, one half of body, one-third of rim, both handles.

Six joining frgts, complete except for head; surface blackened and worn.

Six joining frgts, complete from neck to feet, missing right hand; deep gash over right knee, surface stained purple.

12.1.3. Dimensions

There are three categories of dimensions that are used to measure attributes of artifacts in Corinth: preserved, actual, and restored. Each dimension must first be assessed to determine whether it is **preserved** (i.e. an incomplete dimension; the dimension in so far as the object is preserved), **actual** (i.e. a complete dimension; as it was when the object was made), or **restored** (i.e. a complete dimension is not preserved, but can be estimated by means of a diameter chart or other form of measurement). The appropriate field is then completed for each dimension in the database.

The abbreviations used for dimension measurements are adopted from the style guide of *Hesperia*:

Dimensions

Diam.	diameter
dim.	dimension
H.	height
L.	length
Th.	thickness
W.	width
max.	maximum
p.	preserved
max. p. dim.	maximum preserved dimension, when no other is possible

Enter the number in meters to one place before the decimal and to three places after the decimal. Follow the format below, always keeping the following order of dimensions: H. 0.105, Diam. of foot 0.056, Diam. of rim 0.083.

0.001 = 1 millimeter
0.010 =1 centimeter =10 millimeters
0.100 =10 centimeters =100 millimeters
1.000 = 1 meter = 100 centimeters = 1000 millimeters

Use the following guidelines to determine which dimensions are measured for pottery:

1. 1. If the full profile is preserved, measure the Height, Diameter of foot, Diameter maximum (diameter of body, if greater than rim/lip), and Diameter of lip/rim.
2. If a fragment is preserved and its orientation is clear, measure the Height, Width, and Thickness (if unusual).
3. If a fragment is preserved and its orientation is unclear, measure the Maximum preserved dimension.

12.1.4. Description

For terms used in the DESCRIPTION, see Figs. 25 and 26. The DESCRIPTION field is used to record notes about the shape of the fragment, not its decoration (see §12.1.4) or condition (see §12.1.2). Begin with the bottom, then the top; outside, then in. Describe what the object is, then describe its parts in the following order:

1. Bottom or Base or Foot (Fig. 26a)
2. Resting surface of foot
3. Undersurface of foot: flat, convex, nippled, domed
4. Body (Fig. 26a)
5. Shoulder, if distinct from body
6. Neck, if a closed shape
7. Rim/Lip (Fig 26a): every vessel has a lip (the upper edge of the vessel), but not every vessel has a rim (an articulation or thickening of the mouth of the vessel)
8. Handle (Fig. 26b)
9. For references to parallels for shape, follow the format: "Similar to C-1947-821 (Edwards 1975, Corinth 7.3, p. 31, cat. 31, pls. 2, 44)"

Example: Oinochoe with flaring ring foot, flat undersurface, globular body, short cylindrical neck, outward thickened rim; vertical strap handle, attached to shoulder and rim.

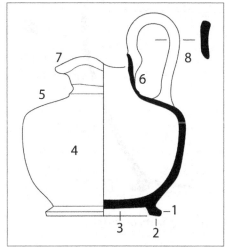

Figure 25. Diagram of an oinochoe. Drawing C. Kolb

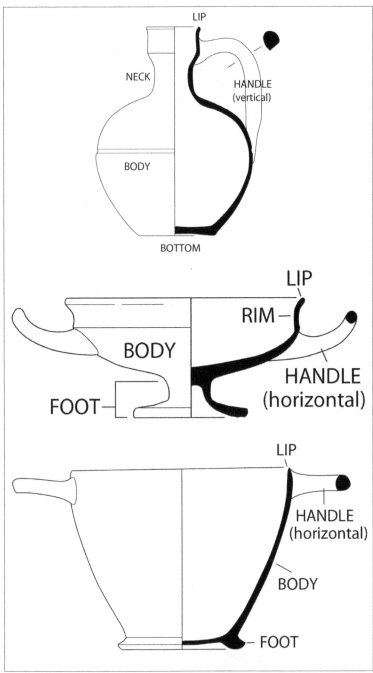

Figure 26a. Nomenclature for describing parts of vessels.

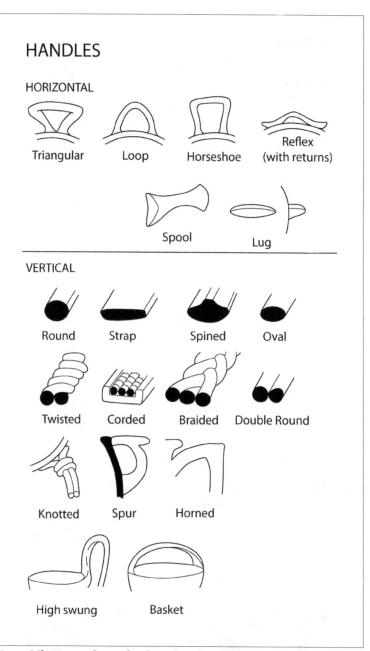

HANDLES

HORIZONTAL

Triangular Loop Horseshoe Reflex (with returns)

Spool Lug

VERTICAL

Round Strap Spined Oval

Twisted Corded Braided Double Round

Knotted Spur Horned

High swung Basket

Figure 26b. Nomenclature for describing handles.

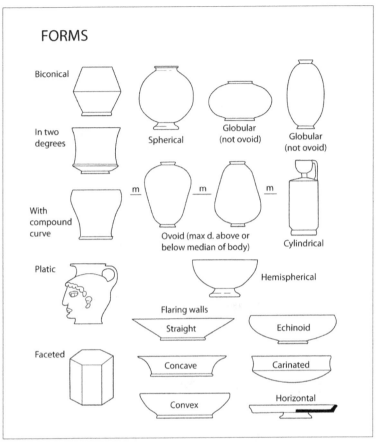

Figure 26c. Nomenclature for describing shapes of vessels.

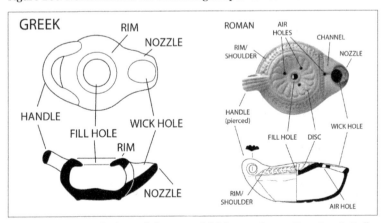

Figure 27. A typical (a) Greek lamp, and (b) Roman lamp. Drawing C. Kolb

12.1.5. Decoration

All painting, incision, relief, wheel-ridging, or other forms of decoration are described in the DECORATION field. Be concise and systematic, describing decorative features from the bottom up, and outside in. For open shapes of Medieval date, in which important decoration exists on the interior, describe the interior first, then the exterior. Complete this field in the following order:

1. Describe grooves or relief decoration: grooves, wheel-ridging, combing, fluting
2. Describe glaze/slip: glaze is generally used for black color on pre-Roman pottery or for vitreous Byzantine decoration; slip is used on Roman pottery
3. Describe painted decoration (note that painted decoration may also have burnishing)
4. Provide references to parallels for decoration, following the format: "Similar to C-1947-821 (Edwards 1975, Corinth 7.3, p. 31, cat. 31, pls. 2, 44)"

Examples:
Black glaze over all.
Bottom half of body reserved, upper half green glazed; black stripe on lip, black stripes on handle back.

12.2. LAMPS

Lamps pose unique challenges to describe because they have various features that are unlike other ceramic objects. The same fields are used in the database to inventory a lamp, but different types of information are required and described below. Only the fabric description and date fields are the same as with other types of pottery finds. If the lamp is not ceramic, then the material (e.g., bronze) needs to be listed in the MATERIAL field. There are differences between Greek and Roman lamps and therefore close attention needs to be paid while inventorying them.

The terms used to describe a lamp are shown in Fig. 27.

12.2.1. Dimensions

For more information on how to take dimension measurements, see §12.1.3. The following dimensions are taken for lamps:

1. Height to rim
2. Maximum height (or height to handle if handle extends above rim)
3. Length from tip of handle to tip of nozzle
4. Diameter of foot and rim

12.2.2. Description

The description for lamps should include the following parts:

1. Mold or handmade
2. General type (e.g. Broneer types [Corinth IV] and Slane [Corinth XVIII.2] if Corinthian; Howland types if classical Athenian; Binder if Roman Athenian)
3. Foot or bottom
4. Body
5. Rim/Shoulder
6. Disc (if Roman)
7. Fill hole
8. Nozzle (and air hole, if Late Roman), wick hole
9. Handle, lug
10. Parallels (follow format for pottery above; see §12.1.4)

Examples:
Greek lamp: Lamp with vertical ring foot, deep convex body, flat rim, large fill hole, long nozzle, flat on top with small wick hole at tip, horizontal strap handle.

Roman Lamp: Lamp with flat bottom, echinoid body, narrow rim, deep concave disc with three fill holes, small air hole at base of short U-shaped nozzle, small wick hole, vertical lug handle, pierced and grooved.

12.2.3. Decoration

Complete the DECORATION field in the following order:

1. Describe relief or impression (if it exists)
2. Describe slip/glaze

12.3. FIGURINES, STATUARY

Like lamps, figurines and statuary have their own specific requirements for inventorying, yet use the same fields in the database. If the figurine or statuette is terracotta, then a fabric description should be included following the instructions below.

12.3.1. Dimensions

For more information about how to take dimension measurements, see §12.1.3. For figurines and statuary, take measurements only for anatomically important features, such as the height of the head, width of the shoulders, etc. If the item is a base, measure the length, width, and height.

12.3.2. Condition

Describe the condition of the item in general terms.

Example:
Six joining frgts., complete from neck to feet, missing right hand; deep gash over right knee; surface stained purple.

12.3.3. Material

Describe the material. If the item is made of marble, do not describe the type of marble unless you are an expert; otherwise, describe the color, crystal size, colored or micaceous veins (if present), and laminating fracture (if present).

12.3.4. Description

Describe the item's form and list any general observations first, then provide details about the item from the top down:

1. Sex, nude or draped, pose, position of legs and arms
2. Details of head and body
3. Drapery
4. Plinth or base
5. Tooling (i.e. use of claw chisel, flat chisel, drill)
6. For figurines: hollow or solid, handmade or moldmade
7. Parallels (follow format for pottery above; see §12.1.4)

Examples:
Figurine of nude standing male, weight on rt. leg, left bent and pulled back, rt. arm raised to scratch head, lt. arm at side. Figure bald, head triangular with closed eyes, long nose, pursed mouth; exaggerated musculature; bare feet.
Female figure, nude, standing with weight on right leg, left turned out, arms at side. Hair worn long, with spirally curls framing forehead, square face, low forehead, thick straight eyebrows, deep set eyes, short nose, pursed lips, short fat neck. Wears a frilly chiton that covers upper arms, over which a diagonal himation, hung from left shoulder, wrapped around waist to hang over extended left forearm. Deep vertical folds fall to feet.

12.3.5. Decoration

Describe painted decoration only, and whether it is systematically presented.

12.4. ARCHITECTURAL TERRACOTTAS

Architectural terracottas refers primarily to tiles, antefixes, and other kinds of roofing materials. They are rarely inventoried unless they are mostly complete or can be associated with a particular structure. This class of object requires a unique method of description, but uses the same database fields as all other objects. The fabric description is necessary and should follow the instructions given below. Refer to Fig. 28 for terms used to describe architectural terracottas.

12.4.1. Pan and Cover Tiles

Select the type of tile from the list below:

PAN AND COVER TILES

Classical Corinthian pan tile	flat floor, triangular sides; undercut at one end for overlap to next tile
Corinthian cover tile	pentagonal in shape
Laconian pan tile	shallow curve with flattened edges
Laconian cover tile	semi-circular in section
Roman Corinthian pan tile	flat with vertical edges along two long sides

12.4.2. Eaves Tile

An eaves tile is the bottommost pan tile at the edge of a roof. It is decorated on the outer face and underside (i.e. the soffit).

12.4.3. Antefix

An antefix is the decorative plaque that covers the bottom-most cover tile. It usually takes the form of a palmette. The antefix that runs along the ridge or apex of the roof is called the "ridge antefix."

12.4.4. Sima

The sima is the gutter that initially runs down either facade along the edge of the roof and turns the corner, ending in a lion-headed spout, before giving way to decorative eaves tiles and antefixes along the flanks. In the 4th century B.C., the sima extended along the long sides, as well. Take care to distinguish between the raking sima (facade) and the lateral sima (flanks).

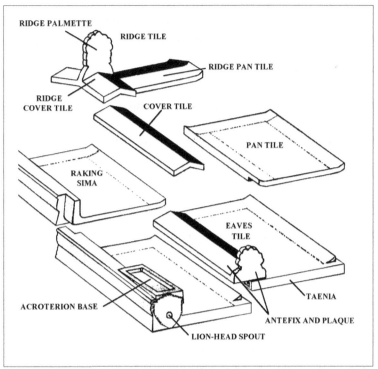

Figure 28. Types of tiles. Drawing J. Herbst.

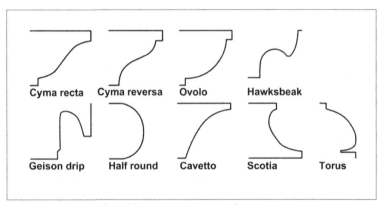

Figure 29. Shapes of moldings. Drawing J. Herbst

12.4.5. Acroterion

The acroterion is the decorative element that falls at the apex of the roof and at the corners. It can simply be a floral motif or a piece of sculpture.

12.4.6. Moldings

Normally moldings are part of the entablature or decorative elements around the base of a building (Fig. 29). At Corinth, they can be made of marble, limestone, or terracotta, as well as some less common materials.

12.5. INSCRIPTIONS

Inscriptions are another unique class of object that requires special instructions for inventorying. The following is intended to help describe a stone inscription, but the method for recording the letters is the standard way that all lettering is described, including graffito on pottery or other objects. The standard database fields are still used but the information required differs from other types of inventorying.

12.5.1. Description

Describe the form of the block: thin, thick, plain, or decorated with moldings. Also describe the treatment of all preserved stone faces (see §12.5.2.).

12.5.2. Tooling

Describe any evidence of tooling: punch (i.e. very coarse point), point-dressed, claw-chisel, smooth, polished, or anathyrosis.

12.5.3. Text

In the WRITING field, type the preserved text in the given language (Greek or Latin). Include uncertain letters in square brackets and illegible letters in square brackets with a period to indicate that an additional letter once existed in this location. Also provide the letter height (Ht.) and the distance between the lines. If finished edges of the stone exist, provide the distance between the edge of the block and the start of the text.

12.6. FABRICS

Part of inventorying any object made of clay is to describe its fabric or, in other words, the nature of the clay from which the object is made. This description should include color, hardness, feel, fracture, and inclusions. If the inclusions can be identified by eye, list them, if not, just describe them using the charts below. When describing fabric examine the entire sherd rather than just a small section. It is not necessary to identify the inclusions for the purposes of basic inventorying, but there are instructions below in case this extra step is taken.

12.6.1. Color

The color of a fresh break should, when possible, be described using natural light and a Munsell Soil Color Chart. Munsell color notations may seem inappropriate, but they follow a system that bridges the cultural idiom of subjective color description. "Yellowish red" defines a specific hue, value, and chroma range within a certain scale, while "buff" applies to a different scale.

Be careful when matching colors. Keep in mind that different people do not have the same capacity for matching a sample to the tabs illustrated, but nearly everyone is capable of placing a color approximately within the three-dimensional scale.

12.6.2. Hardness

Hardness should be determined based on a modified Moh's scale (below) and assessed with a fingernail and knife tip. In actuality, this is not a hardness test, but rather a test of cohesiveness. Firing and soil conditions both affect mineral cohesion; a sherd from the forum at Corinth may be judged as "very hard," while a sherd of the same fabric from the Demeter Sanctuary may be "very soft."

The modified Moh's scale values are as follows:

Very Soft	fingernail scratches easily
Soft	fingernail scratches
Medium hard	penknife scratches
Hard	penknife just scratches
Very hard	penknife will not scratch

12.6.3. Appearance

The appearance of a fresh break is an indicator of hardness and content of the ceramic body and may be suggestive of the technology used to produce it. Granular fractures tend to have numerous large inclusions, while smooth breaks tend to have few or no inclusions.

Select from the following options to describe the appearance of the break (Fig. 30):

Laminar	platy, stepped appearance
Hackly	large, angular irregularities
Granular	fine, more rounded irregularities
Conchoidal	large, smooth, angular facets similar to chert
Smooth	even, without apparent irregularities

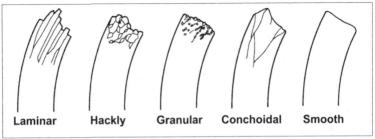

Figure 30. Appearance of breaks.

12.6.4. Feel

A description of how the surface (as opposed to the break) "feels" is useful and complements a description of the appearance. The terms suggested below can be used in conjunction with each other; it is possible for a sherd to be both harsh and powdery (as with Late Roman Palestinian amphoras), smooth and greasy (Middle Bronze Age "Minyan Ware"), or rough and greasy (Early Bronze Age "Talc Ware"). This attribute is another indicator of cohesiveness and content.

Harsh	abrasive surface
Rough	angular irregularies present
Smooth	no irregularities discernible
Greasy	slick, almost slippery surface
Powdery	grainy feel, often leaving powder on finger

12.6.5. Inclusions

Inclusions are a valuable attribute for identifying and characterizing pottery. They consist of any material within the clay that is naturally occurring or is added during the manufacturing process. Inclusions need to be described as carefully as the above features of a sherd, and can be done so even more systematically.

12.6.6. Frequency

A verbal estimate of the frequency of inclusions can be made using a frequency chart (Fig. 31). It is important to keep in mind that inclusion size affects the perception of frequency. An estimate of size and frequency should be given for all inclusions contained within the new break before describing the size and frequency of individual types of inclusions.

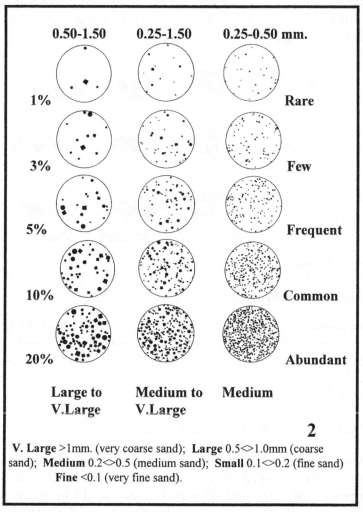

Figure 31. Modified Udden-Wentworth

12.6.7. Shape and Roundness of Inclusions

A description of the shape and roundness of inclusions can be made by consulting Fig. 32, which illustrates the gradations from rounded to angular grains on one axis, and from spherical to platy on the other. Keep in mind that the observed surface presents only two dimensions of a three-dimensional object, such that a cylindrical object may appear tubular, spherical, or oval in cross-section. Only a simple subjective color notation is necessary: for example, brown or white, qualified by adjectives such as milky, vitreous, or glassy.

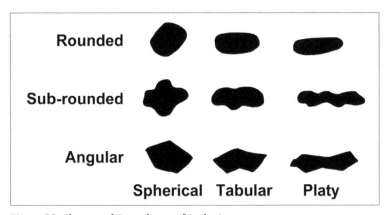

Figure 32. Shape and Roundness of inclusions

12.6.8. Identification

Inclusions are usually too small to identify with any certainty in a hand specimen; however, an accurate description is of far greater value than an incorrect identification. One may, however, make a qualified guess after a thoroughout description.

Table for identification of inclusions:

I. Inclusions that react with dilute hydrochloric acid.
When these inclusions are exposed to dilute (5%) hydrochloric acid, they will effervesce. Care should be taken to observe that the reaction is taking place on the inclusion

itself rather than with the surrounding clay matrix, which may be of a calcareous nature.

Shell	long curved structures, sometimes an observable lamination
Ooliths	spherical or slightly ovoid, sometimes-concentric banding
Limestone	irregular to rounded
Calcite	white or clear vitreous inclusions, sometimes rhomb-shaped

II. Inclusions that do not react with dilute hydrochloric acid. These inclusions can include mineral and rock fragments. The classification is divided into light- and dark-colored inclusions.

A. Light-colored minerals:

Mica	glistening flakes
Quartz/Quartzite	clear/white vitreous grains, very hard
Sandstone	aggregate of white vitreous grains
Dolomite	dull white grains or rhombs, medium hard
Feldspar	dull milky white to orange/pink grains, hard
Chert	range of colors, light to dark, very hard, can show conchoidal fracture

B. Dark-colored minerals:

Mica	glistening flakes
Mudstone or Grog	range of colors (brown/grey/red), usually slightly elongate and subangular
Fe-Ti oxide, ferro-magnesian silicate, rock fragment	black grains
Chert	range of colors, light to dark, very hard, can show conchoidal fracture

III. Heterogeneous inclusions that do not react with dilute hydrochloric acid.

| Rock fragments | composed of a number of grains, variable colors |

12.6.9. Voids

Voids can be confusing for the non-specialist, especially when it comes to differentiating between vughs, vesicles, channels, and chambers (see Fig. 33). If the voids can be seen using a hand lens, they are probably vughs or vesicles. An estimated percentage of the visible surface area made up of voids—expressed verbally rather than numerically—is useful and simple to assess. The orientation of voids relative to the surfaces of the pottery should be recorded: e.g. parallel, inclined (approximate angle if possible), or no preferred orientation.

Planar voids	thin elongated voids
Vesicles	smooth, spherical voids
Cross sections of channels	rounded voids
Vughs (divide into large [2–3 mm] and fine [less than 1 mm long] scale)	irregularly shaped voids

12.6.10. Porosity

An estimation of porosity can be quantified with the help of a domestic oven. The sherds should be heated at 105° C for one hour and weighed dry of unassociated water. The sherds are then immersed in water for 24 hours and reweighed after having dried the surface. The difference in weight represents the water retained in the open pores and can be expressed as a percentage of the dry weight.

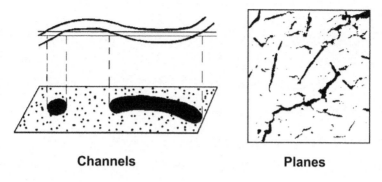

Channels   **Planes**

Figure 31. Examples of (a) channels, and (b) planes

13. ADDITIONAL NOTES ON SAMPLING

The most important aspect of developing a sampling strategy is to understand how the information gained from the sample will enhance knowledge of the period or any issues in question (i.e. the aims) for the site or area of interest. Asking key questions—or targeting specific information (i.e. objectives) that will contribute to a greater understanding of the past—will clarify which tasks must be carried out to achieve these aims. It is impossible to make decisions about the most effective way to sample, how best to deploy resources, or how to modify the approach in response to issues that may arise if the aims and objectives of the project are unclear. Flexibility in response to new information or changing circumstances is an important part of project planning and management. This makes it possible to modify the aims and objectives as a project progresses. The need for sampling and a consideration of what types of samples will best address the project's aims should be considered at the start of the project (see the table below). Advice should be sought from appropriate specialists to ensure that the sampling strategy will meet the project's needs and be cost-effective. The project design must demonstrate that the sampling strategy is fit for its purpose. A well-constructed sampling strategy addresses the aims and objectives of the project and includes random contexts that are selected so as to be mathematically rigorous and avoid missing important deposits by sampling in a statistically random manner. It is vital that the excavator systematically and randomly sample to ensure that the whole site is considered and to avoid missing unusual contexts, as well as choose an agreed-upon sampling strategy that can be easily re-evaluated if additional and unexpected contexts require sampling.

Open-area excavation is not fully compatible with the expectations of geoarchaeologists, who prefer to work with preserved stratigraphic columns starting at the modern surface. This is because geoarchaeologists usually are not on site all the time. As a result, even in a trench-and-balk system, the geoarchaeological samples can only be taken from sections determined before excavation begins or from sections created for a specific feature, such as a room or pit. The ideal situation in an open-area excavation is for the team to include a geoarchaeologist who is present throughout the excavation. This team member will be instrumental in helping to develop a sampling strategy that targets the kinds of information that will enhance the interpretation of the site as well as to modify the strategy to deal with developing circumstances as excavation progresses.

Sampling Method	Pros and Cons
Random	Mathematically ideal, but will miss many (if not most) of the most significant deposits. Can be conducted on the analyzed whole.
Judgment	Samples the seemingly significant deposits but misses those that are less obviously significant. Can be conducted on the analyzed whole.
Systematic	Methodologically ideal, but costly.

13.1. SOIL SAMPLES FOR NON-WATER FLOTATION

Do not wash sherds or pots that are destined for organic analysis. Adhering soil should be preserved. If there is no adhering soil, then a sample from the immediate area should be bagged separately.

A minimum ceramic sample size required for lipid extraction is ca. 2 grams. For visible residues, only a small amount of the residue is required, but multiple samples should be taken from different parts of the residue and bagged separately.

Contamination is always a concern. In soil samples, contamination comes primarily from **wind, plants, soil, and animals (including humans).** It is preferable, therefore, to take samples on calm days in order to minimize contamination via the wind. If you must sample on windy days, attempt to shelter the sampling area during the sampling process and conduct the sampling as quickly as possible. As excavation proceeds, the soil that is removed becomes a potential source of contamination for archaeological surfaces as they are exposed.

All samples must be marked with the context number, and a Sample Sheet **must be completed.**

13.2. SAMPLE COLLECTION PROCEDURES FOR PHYTOLITHS

Follow the steps below to collect samples for phytolith analysis:

1. Using a trowel free of dirt, scrape the area to be sampled to remove the accumulation of modern pollen.
2. Clean the trowel of dirt. Spray the trowel with distilled water and wipe with a paper towel.
3. Quickly remove a phytolith sample (approximately 200 cc or 1 cup), place in a resealable bag, and secure. If taken from a section, take the sample from as narrow a horizontal band as possible without crossing boundaries with other strata. In thick deposits greater than 5 cm, horizontal samples may be taken every 2 cm. Double-bag the sample.

13.3. WET SAMPLES

If a waterlogged sample is taken, it should be kept wet. Pack it carefully in a clean plastic container or three well-sealed polyethylene bags, leaving as small an air space as possible.

13.4. RADIOCARBON (C¹⁴) SAMPLES

Samples to be used for radiocarbon dating must be collected and packed carefully to avoid contamination from dirt and modern packing materials. Make sure to wear clean, disposable plastic gloves. The tools and containers that will come in contact with the sample should be free of all organic matter, grease, oils, lubricants, preservatives, etc. Only tweezers with flat, smooth blades should be used, as those with ridged blades can introduce contaminants.

To collect the sample, use a clean metal spatula or tweezers to lift it out of the ground. Remove as much adhering dirt and small roots as possible, place it on a clean piece of aluminum foil, and gently fold the foil around it. Place the foil in a self-sealing polyethylene bag and label the bag with the sample's context number. The minimum sample size necessary for materials to be collected for dating is around 10 gr.

13.5. SEED SAMPLES

Seeds are often found carbonized with a great deal of structural detail still preserved. If seeds are to be used for radiocarbon dating, the strict sampling procedure outlined above should be used.

More frequently, however, seeds are recovered through dry or wet sieving or flotation of soil samples. Depending on the size of the sieve used, quantities of small seeds as well as other plant remains can be recovered. If large quantities of seeds are visible in the soil, a sample should be taken for flotation. In such cases, it is best to avoid dry sieving, as this will rattle seeds against each other and against lumps of dirt, causing the seeds to break.

A sample taken from flotation should be left out to dry (never in the sun). The risk of microbiological growth is high if the sample is packed wet.

14. FIELD CONSERVATION

Every material has a stable form in relation to the environment in which it exists. When buried, an object is surrounded by a new microclimate—possibly one that is vastly different from its previous state. The material comprising the object will begin to adapt to these new conditions. Assuming these conditions are reasonably constant, the material will undergo a process of modification to approach a stable relationship, or equilibrium, with the new environment. As the material approaches equilibrium, the rate of change will decrease, eventually ceasing when equilibrium is reached. This stability will remain constant as long as the object remains buried in the ground. In a burial environment, materials are broken down by physical, chemical, and/or biological processes.

The extent to which the material is modified from its original state during the period burial depends mainly on the soil and climatic conditions that prevail, as well as how the material behaves under those particular conditions. Agents that contribute to the deterioration/decay process are water, oxygen, acidity and alkalinity of the soil, salts, temperature, organisms, animals, and plants. Change will resume as soon as an object is uncovered and is suddenly exposed to new environmental conditions. From the very moment the object is exposed to air, the processes of deterioration and corrosion begin anew. Some materials are more sensitive than others to these changes, such as textiles, wood, bone, leather, skin, and fibers.

When such objects are recovered, careful handling, packing, and storage ensure that these unique objects are more likely to reach the conservator unchanged. Micro-excavation of the dirt and corrosion products attached to an object should be carried out in the conservation laboratory to reveal details of composition, function, and structure. Careless cleaning may destroy information that could be revealed in the laboratory.

The presence of a conservator is essential throughout the entire excavation period.

| NEVER ATTEMPT TO CLEAN OBJECTS ON SITE |

14.1. GENERAL INSTRUCTIONS

Labeling: Labels should be resistant to physical and chemical damage, biodeterioration, and the action of solvents.

Packaging: Individual bagging or boxing (with cushioning for smaller finds) in a controlled microclimate is generally preferred and can be achieved with the use of plastic boxes and a moisture-absorbent material such as silica gel and acid-free paper. Never pack materials using tobacco tins, matchboxes, cigarette boxes, tin boxes, brown paper bags, biscuit tins, cotton, wool, newspaper, toilet paper, or colored tissue.

Materials found wet should be kept wet in order to prevent irreversible physical damage, which occurs upon drying (never re-wet dried out waterlogged organic materials). If waterlogged materials are to be kept wet for some period, a biocide should be added to the water to prevent microorganism growth. The water may be replaced when the object reaches the conservation laboratory. Never wrap objects, as unwrapping is always damaging. Generally, a key guideline is to keep the material's immediate environment as close as possible to its burial conditions.

Small Objects: Small objects should be transferred to the museum in boxes or bags.

Large Objects: Large objects may need to be cushioned using polythene foam, bubble pack, or soil freshly sieved from the excavation.

Stones: A large stone object should be placed in a basket, bucket, or any other suitable container so that it may be handled and moved without damaging its surface.

Ceramics: Pot sherds should be washed and left in the shade to dry. If an unusual material is noticed on the surface (e.g. unfired color-substance), set the sherd aside. Never soak sherds in water, especially from prehistoric deposits, because most of the time they are not well fired. These sherds should be treated differently and cleaned under the supervision of a conservator.

Figurines: Figurines are painted. Never wet or wash them at the site, as traces of colors can be easily removed.

Glass: Before lifting a piece of glass, clean around it carefully with a wooden spatula or soft brush to remove all surrounding dirt. Do not use metal tools, as they will scratch the surface of the glass. Be careful not to detach any iridescent layers from the surface; if necessary, leave some of the dirt adhering to the glass to protect these thin layers. Once the object is loosened from the dirt, place it in a padded container. Keep the glass in a cool place away from direct sunlight, and take it to the conservation laboratory at the earliest opportunity.

Organic Materials: Keep all organic materials in the shade. Call the conservator.

Metals: All metals—with the exception of gold—are unstable and corrode when combined with other elements, such as oxygen, sulfur, carbon, phosphorous, and chlorine. First remove the surrounding dirt. If the metal object appears stable, carefully undercut it and place it on a padded container. If the object looks broken or unstable, call the conservator.

Gold: Pure gold is durable and resistant to corrosion, but other metals present in the alloy will corrode. If the corrosion is extensive, it can be difficult at times to recognize excavated gold. Copper corrosion products, for example, can completely cover a gold object, making it appear green as if it is a corroded piece of bronze. When alloyed with silver, a pale-colored metal is produced. If the amount of silver approaches 30 percent, the alloy is almost white. The addition of copper produces a reddish gold.

Gold or gold alloy objects may be very weak structurally and will crack or break with careless or excessive handling. An object of this material can be removed from the ground only after the surrounding dirt is carefully removed. When the object it is completely loose, carefully undercut the object, gently lift it out of the ground, and place it into a padded container.

Gold may also be encountered as a very soft, thin foil (e.g. folded leaves in wreaths). Do not attempt to unfold gold foil. Transfer the material to a conservation lab immediately.

14.2. EXPLANATIONS FOR ARTIFACT DETERIORATION

Iron:

Appearance	Likely Occurrence
Orange-brown corrosion products mixed with brown soil deposits and encrusted with grit and small stones	Most aerated burial conditions
White to light grey coating	Usually from chalk soils
Black deposit, often with fine fragments of organic material	Residue of burnt organic materials
Deep orange/red, even corrosion layer	Possibly due to burning
Black coat of even texture, possibly with blue patches	From anaerobic, usually waterlogged strata, often with phosphatic material present
Bright orange protuberances; object very light in weight	Usually from well-aerated strata

Silver:

Appearance	Likely Occurrence
Metallic with dull yellow tarnish	Rare; occurs in favorable burial conditions; more common in dry climates
Dull grey/white surface, turns a dull lilac color when excavated	Usually from damp, oxygenated environments
Green patches or totally green	Alloyed with copper
Black, smooth surface layer	Very common in waterlogged and non-waterlogged environments

Copper and Copper Alloys:

Appearance	Likely Occurrence
Smooth, shiny, dark green surface with good preservation of surface detail	Favorable burial conditions
Soft light green corrosion and hard dark green warts; surface detail obscured and object fragile	Aggressive burial environments
Green corrosion and brown soil deposits	Ubiquitous
Surface often susceptible to physical damage, revealing light green powder beneath	Flaking often occurs following excavation and is due to active corrosion
Solid black, smooth surface or shiny metallic surface with black patches	Waterlogged deposits
Object covered in blue sugar-like crystals	Dry environments

Likely occurrence of totally or partially mineralized organic remains on iron and copper alloy objects.

Object	Source Of Organics
Swords	Handles, scabbards (wood, bone, ivory, leather, fleece)
Tools	Handles (predominantly wood but possibly bone or horn)
Buckles, strap ends, lace points	Remains of textile or leather are often located inside the strap end or points
Grave goods	Textiles, leather, insect remains, skin, fibers
Tacks, studs, nails, clamps	Wood from boxes, coffins, structures; textile and leather from clothing or armor
Iron pipe collars	Wooden pipes
Iron hobnails	Leather from shoes

15. BIBLIOGRAPHY

Barker, P. 1997. *Techniques of Archaeological Excavation*, 2nd ed., New York.

Broneer, O. 1930. *Corinth* IV.2: *Terracotta Lamps*, Cambridge.

Dever, W. G., and H. D. Lance. 1978. *A Manual of Field Excavation: Handbook for Field Archaeologists*, New York.

Folk, R. 1988. *Petrology of Sedimentary Rocks*, Austin.

Harris, E. 1975. "The Stratigraphic Sequence: A Question of Time," *World Archaeology* 7, pp. 109-121.

Harris, E. 1989. *Principles of Archaeological Stratigraphy*, New York.

Hodgson, J. 1974. *Soil Survey Field Handbook: Describing and Sampling Soil Profiles*, Harpenden.

Munsell Color, 1994. *Munsell Soil Color Charts*, rev. ed., New Windsor, NY.

Munsterberg, M. 2008-2009. "Visual Description," http://writingaboutart.org/pages/visualdesc.html.

Robinson, H. and S. Weinberg. 1960. "Excavations at Corinth, 1959," *Hesperia* 29, 225-253.

Roksandic, M. 200.3 "New Standardised Visual Forms for Recording the Presence of Human Skeletal Elements in Archaeological and Forensic Contexts," *Internet Archaeology* 13. http://dx.doi.org/10.11141/ia.13.3

Slane, K. 1990. *Corinth* XVIII.2: *The Sanctuary of Demeter and Kore: The Roman Pottery and Lamps*, Princeton.

Spence C., 1994. *Archaeological Site Manual*, 3rd ed., London.

Wheeler, M. 1954. *Archaeology from the Earth*, Oxford.

16. GLOSSARY OF TERMS

Abutment: An intersection of wall where the stones of the two walls do not overlap or intermix; the end of one wall is built against the face of the other.

Agricultural plow zone: The layer of the soil affected by agricultural plowing of cultivated lands.

Alluvial deposits: Soil deposited by running water, such as streams, rivers, and flood waters.

Andesite: A dark, fine-grained, brown or greyish volcanic rock that is intermediate in composition between rhyolite and basalt.

Arbitrary trench: Placement of a trench within a defined area of excavation, such as a sample unit that is defined by a site grid, has no specific cultural relevance, and is placed at the prerogative of the excavator.

Ashlar: Masonry made of large square-cut stones, typically used as a facing on walls of brick or stone.

Associated objects: Contexts or objects deposited at or around the same time.

Balks: A strip of earth left between excavation trenches for the study of the complete stratigraphy of a site.

Bonding material: Adhesive material (e.g. concrete, mortar, adobe) that joins two objects together.

Bone stack: A pile of bones composed of parts of possibly multiple individuals in secondary or tertiary burial.

Bricks (fired): A block of refractory ceramic material constructed primarily to withstand high temperatures and to have low conductivity.

Built floor: A purposely constructed surface found within a defined architectural space.

Built hearth: A fireplace lined with material such as clay, brick, or stone and used for heating and cooking.

Built road: A purposely constructed, improved surface used primarily as a thoroughfare for foot or animal traffic between two places.

Carbonized organics: Charred plant or seed particulates often found in burned contexts or recovered during water flotation.

Cartesian coordinate system: Coordinate system that specifies each point uniquely in a plane by a pair of numerical coordinates, which are the signed distances to the point from two fixed perpendicular directed lines, measured in the same unit of length.

Cement: A powdery substance made with calcined lime and clay; it is mixed with water to form mortar, or mixed with sand, gravel, and water to make concrete.

Cist pit: A hole cut into subterranean context that is prepared and lined with a masonry or rock intended to be used as a grave.

Clay: Fine-grained soil that combines minerals, metal oxides, and organic matter in a plastic state that changes consistency when wet or dry.

Clear boundary: A clearly demarcated divide between strata or contexts.

Coarse-grained: Strongly cemented sediment that cannot be broken apart with one's hands.

Conglomerate: Sedimentary rock composed of rounded pebbles and sediments (sand) that are cemented together by geologic processes; a very common type at Corinth.

Contamination: Materials that are not part of a natural archaeological deposit or assemblage but which have intruded or altered the deposit or assemblage.

Context: The remains of a unique, definable, and individual stratigraphic event.

Context number: A unique number assigned, site-wide, to a specific context such as a floor assemblage, floor surface, road, feature, etc., which is kept in a separate, sequential registry.

Context register: The list of individual and unique context numbers and their descriptions.

Corinthian roof tile: Molded, flat, pan terracotta roof tile with pitched roof tile placed atop.

Course: A continuous horizontal layer of similarly sized building material usually found within in a wall; most often made of cut or modified stone.

Cover tile: A semi-cylindrical roofing tile, much like a half-pipe which is laid over the joints of flat roofing tiles with raised edges.

Cross section: Exposure of a deposit vertically to reveal the stratigraphy of a particular feature.

Cut: A negative feature that is evidence of an anthropomorphic activity that removed soil or another context (e.g. the digging of a pit); a cut cannot be excavated, only observed.

Cyclopean: Type of ancient masonry made with massive irregular blocks.

Deposit: A single event of a deposit of sediment that may have been caused naturally (e.g. alluvial) or culturally (e.g. leveling fill).

Diamond tile: A terracotta tile used during the Roman period at Corinth.

Diffuse boundary: A diffuse or unclear boundary between strata or contexts.

Disarticulated skeleton: Human remains that are no longer in correct anatomical position.

Disturbance: Any cultural or natural event that modifies artifacts in an archaeological context.

Drain: An object such as a pipe or conduit from which liquid withdraws or outflows.

Dry sieving: Mesh held in a frame used to separate coarse from fine particles; used to separate and collect artifacts from sediments.

Dumped fill: Purposely deposited material (sediments) often used to fill or level an area.

Dumped rubble: Purposely deposited material rock or construction debris.

Elevation: The vertical distance above or below an arbitrarily defined standard or datum.

Excavation Notes field: A field on context recording sheets for taking notes that capture additional information observed by the excavator that will help in interpretation; meant to provide more thorough interpretation and answer "why" questions that go above and beyond simple description.

Figurine: A small three-dimensional object intended to represent a human, animal, or other object; possibly made out of a variety of materials, but most often clay at Corinth.

Floor: A purposely constructed surface inside or associated with a structure which is constructed by earth, plaster, mosaic, rock, or slab; it differs from a surface (see below).

Foundation trench: A linear cutting that is part of a pre-wall construction and that can be filled with debris; meant to hold the wall foundation.

Glass tessera: An individual glass tile, usually formed into a cube or rectilinear shape, made of glass that was used in the creation of a mosaic.

Grave cut: A negative feature context that represents a moment in time when a deposit was removed for the creation of a pit intended for human remains.

Grave fill: Sediments that cover over and fill the space that contains a burial.

Half-sectioning: Procedure to excavate a complex area by dividing a context in half and excavating one side stratigraphically; this also produces a vertical section of the context in question.

Harris Matrix: A tool used to depict the temporal succession of archaeological contexts and thus the sequence of depositions and surfaces on a "dry land" archaeological site, otherwise called a "stratigraphic sequence."

HATT projection: A geodetic system once used in Greece that is now out of date, based on geodetic data points.

Hydroplaster: Waterproof plaster that is normally used on the interior of a cistern or other feature that is intended to hold water.

In situ: Translates to "on site," "in position," or "in place;" it refers to an artifact that has not been moved from its original place of deposition.

Lesbian masonry: Characterized by stone polygonal masonry blocks in the facing of walls; probably with stylistic origins from the island of Lesbos, as a particular stone that is native to the island fractures in a slightly curvilinear fashion.

Leveling fill: Loose sediments or rubble purposely dumped into an area or atop a surface as a means of creating a flat or level surface.

Limestone: A sedimentary rock composed mainly of skeletal fragments of marine organisms such as coral and mollusks.

Line weight: The relative weight (strength, heaviness, or darkness) of a drawn line against a background.

Lot: A group of individual contexts that can be meaningfully grouped together as an archaeologically understandable feature (e.g. a series of contexts in a pit); these contexts would be assigned a lot number .

Manhole: A small covered opening in a floor, pavement, or other surface meant to allow a person to enter a subterranean area.

Marble: Metamorphic rock composed of recrystallized carbonate minerals such as calcite or dolomite; often used as a term to describe metamorphosed limestone.

Masonry: Stone, brick, or concrete used as building material.

Maximum dimensions: The greatest, largest, or widest possible measurement of archaeological data (e.g. of an artifact, structure, or context).

Metaled road: Compact, hard-trodden feature associated with heavy use atop a road surface.

Mixed course (masonry): A horizontal band of masonry made up of either mixed materials and/or uneven height and placement.

Mixed soil/sediment: Descriptor for soils that possess more than one distinct color component, particularly with respect to surrounding soil contexts.

Modern cement: Binder used in construction that sets and hardens in order to hold materials together; often lime-based.

Mud-plaster: A composite of fine clay sediments and fibers used to provide protection, smoothing, and insulation to building floors and walls.

Mud brick: A brick made of loam, mud, and sand that is tempered by vegetal fiber.

Open area: A method of excavation where large areas of the site are cleared in such a manner that balks are not preserved; contexts are excavated across a wide area and an attempt is made to stay within single chronological horizons as the excavation proceeds.

Orientation: The relative physical position or direction of something; the alignment or direction of an object it faces or is aligned with.

Pedestal: 1. An excavation technique in which excavated objects are left in place atop columns of soils while the surrounding area is excavated. 2. The base of a structure, especially one supporting a statue or monumental column.

Pier: A freestanding, rectangular mass of masonry supporting the superstructure of a building, such as a roof.

Pit: An excavated hole into surrounding context(s) usually of soil; used for storage, refuse disposal, etc.

Plaster: A mixture of sediment (often calcium carbonate) used to cover a vertical or horizontal surface.

Platform: A raised, level surface on which an object or person might be placed or might stand.

Primary burial: The initial or direct inhumation of fully articulated skeletal remains.

Primary deposition or inclusion: An undisturbed original deposition of an archaeological context (e.g. a grave or a floor deposit); these are very rare in archaeology.

Quarter-section: Excavation in quadrants; a procedure used to excavate areas in four quarters, often starting with two diagonally opposite quadrants in a manner that preserves two or more stratigraphic profiles.

Quoins: Masonry blocks at the corner of a wall (see Fig. 21).

Ramp: A sloping surface that connects two levels with an incline.

Random course: A masonry (e.g. bricks, stone, etc.) layer without regular placement or horizontal alignment (see Fig. 21).

Reflective prism: An optical refraction mirror (often attached to a stadia rod) used in conjunction with a total station in order to take measurements.

Regular course: A masonry (e.g. bricks, stone, etc.) layer that is placed systemically at a regular and consistent height (see Fig. 21).

Representative elevations: When a new context is excavated, elevations (in relation to a known datum point) that are recorded that typify key elevations of an artifact, context, etc.

Revetment: An elaborate addition to a wall or floor; often of flat, even pieces of marble or another special stone and typically covering a simpler floor of packed earth or cement or a partially-plastered wall; most common in the Roman period at Corinth.

Road: A prepared surface that leads from one place to another.

Robbing trench: 1. A trench that originally contained the foundation of a wall but from which the stones have been removed. 2. A trench excavated by looters.

Sarcophagus: A sepulchral chest made of stone (marble), wood, or pottery.

Scarp: The inner side of a ditch below the parapet of a fortification.

Secondary burial: The practice of removing the remains of a human to another grave or ossuary at a second location, often after the remains had decayed to skeletal material.

Secondary context: An archaeological deposit that is no longer in its original position but has been disturbed and moved through natural or human action.

Section: A view of the archaeological sequence in a vertical plane or cross section that shows stratigraphic layering.

Sharp boundary: Clear or distinct delineation between contexts.

Sieve: Also called a screen; a container with a mesh-lined bottom (of varying size) which is used to separate large particles (i.e. artifacts) from sediments.

Skin balk: Protective strip of soil left around a later context while an earlier context is being excavated .

Slope degree: The estimate of the degree to which the surface slopes.

Slump: The deformation of a context out of its original position through natural processes such as settling or subsidence.

Soil condition: Description of soil characteristics (e.g. dry, moist), the circumstances around its excavation (e.g. the length of time the soil has been exposed to the environment), and additional data related to excavation methods (e.g. whether the soil was sprayed down, etc.).

Sorting: The distribution of inclusions found in sediments; the degree of sorting is a measure of the frequency at which particles of the same size occur.

Stone tessera: A stone shaped into a square or rectangular tile to be used in the creation of a mosaic.

Stratum(a): A layer of material, naturally or artificially formed, that is part of the geological or archaeological record.

Stratigraphic relationship: The order by which strata are deposited and how they interact with one another in the archaeological record.

Stratigraphy: Archaeological/geological principle that natural and cultural events deposit like strata (sediments, ash, etc.) of material in discernable layers.

String course: A horizontal band or coarse of masonry or brick in a wall.

Stylobate: A continuous base supporting a row of columns.

Tertiary context: An archaeological context that has been heavily disturbed, perhaps moved from its original depositional context two or more times before its final deposit.

Terminus ante quem: "Time before which;" the latest possible date for an artifact or context.

Terminus post quem: "Time after which;" the earliest possible date for an artifact or context.

Thrown pottery: Pottery samples that, after some degree of analysis and recording, are discarded.

Title tag: The essential summary of the context that includes key words or phrases that both define and describe the deposit as succinctly as possible .

Top plan: A drawing or diagram created from the top, or horizontal, view; also known as a plan map.

Topsoil: The typically highly fertile, agricultural, uppermost layer of soil.

Total station: An instrument that uses optics and an electronic distance measure to read slope and distances from the instrument to a particular point (usually sighted with a prism).

Truncation: The cutting off of a portion of an artifact, context, surface, etc.

Uncoursed: Typically rough, unhewn construction stone stacked in an irregular fashion, with no identifiable horizontal layers (see Fig. 21).

Vertical section: Also known as a cross section; reveals the strata and stratigraphic relationships of a particular deposit.

Wall foundation: Masonry, cut stone, concrete, or rubble walls below ground level that serve as the main support for a wall structure.

Wall repair: Clear patched or filled portion of wall that indicates historic modification or repair.

Wall superstructure: The portion of a wall (often masonry or stone) that exists above ground level.

Water flotation: Use of water and fine mesh to process soil or feature fill in order to recover small and/or organic artifacts.

Wellhead: A superstructure placed over a well.

Well: An excavated structure created by digging, boring, or drilling into the earth to access subterranean water resources.

Wentworth Scale: Scale of measurement used to classify and measure particle size of sediment.

Wheeler Boxes: Grid system of systematic digging whereby the field is divided into small squares and each square is clearly separated by a narrow balk that is never excavated; this method permits an area to be excavated but preserves a vertical cross-section that reveals the strata of the site as the trench is dug; pioneered by Mortimer Wheeler.

Appendix: Sheets and Forms

The following appendix contains the various sheets and forms mentioned in the text. Downloadable, full-sized versions of these forms are available at this link (https://perma.cc/35EF-LREC) or at the QR code below.

1. Cut Sheet
2. Deposit Sheet
3. Drawing Sheet
4. Sample Sheet
5. Skeleton Sheet
6. Structure Sheet
6. Working Harris Matrix Sheet

| TITLE TAG (6.3.1) | CONTEXT NUMBER |

CUT   RECORDED BY

RECORDING DATE

COORDINATES (6.3.2)

| | N | | S | | E | | W |

ELEVATIONS (6.3.3)

TOP   BOTTOM

SHAPE IN PLAN (6.3.4)

| ORIENTATION (6.3.10) | DIMENSIONS (6.3.5) |

| BREAK OF SLOPE - TOP (6.3.6) | BREAK OF SLOPE – BASE (6.3.8) |

| SIDES (6.3.7) | BASE (6.3.9) |

HARRIS MATRIX (6.3.12)

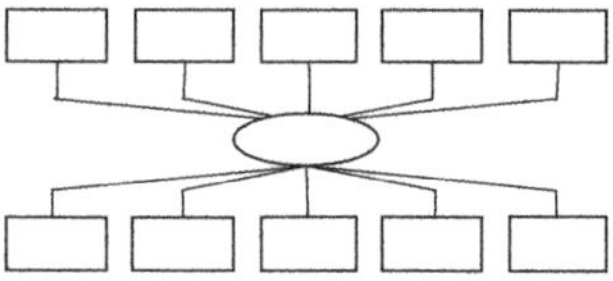

FILLED BY (6.3.13)

TRUNCATION (6.3.11)

FORMATION/INTERPRETATION (6.2.12)

DRAWINGS (4)
☐ TOP PLAN   ☐ SECTION   ☐ OTHER

PHOTOGRAPHS (5)

Cut Sheet
Page 1

CORINTH EXCAVATIONS
AMERICAN SCHOOL OF CLASSICAL STUDIES AT ATHENS

NOTES (6.3.14)

Notes Continue?
☐ Yes ☐ No

Cut Sheet
Page 2

157

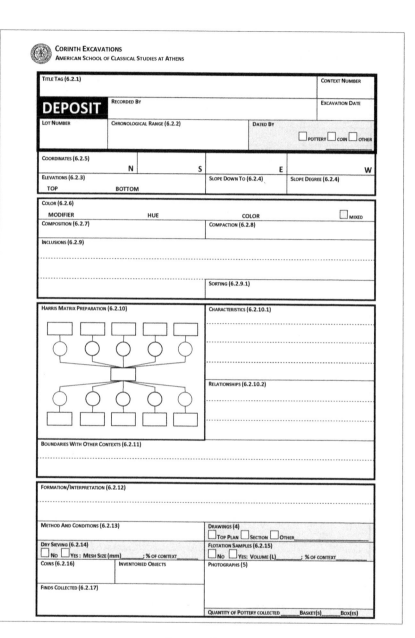

CORINTH EXCAVATIONS
AMERICAN SCHOOL OF CLASSICAL STUDIES AT ATHENS

TITLE TAG (6.2.1)

DEPOSIT

CONTEXT NUMBER

RECORDED BY

EXCAVATION DATE

LOT NUMBER

CHRONOLOGICAL RANGE (6.2.2)

DATED BY

☐ POTTERY ☐ COIN ☐ OTHER

COORDINATES (6.2.5)

N   S   E   W

ELEVATIONS (6.2.3)

TOP   BOTTOM

SLOPE DOWN TO (6.2.4)   SLOPE DEGREE (6.2.4)

COLOR (6.2.6)

MODIFIER   HUE   COLOR   ☐ MIXED

COMPOSITION (6.2.7)   COMPACTION (6.2.8)

INCLUSIONS (6.2.9)

SORTING (6.2.9.1)

HARRIS MATRIX PREPARATION (6.2.10)   CHARACTERISTICS (6.2.10.1)

RELATIONSHIPS (6.2.10.2)

BOUNDARIES WITH OTHER CONTEXTS (6.2.11)

FORMATION/INTERPRETATION (6.2.12)

METHOD AND CONDITIONS (6.2.13)   DRAWINGS (4)

☐ TOP PLAN ☐ SECTION ☐ OTHER

DRY SIEVING (6.2.14)   FLOTATION SAMPLES (6.2.15)

☐ NO ☐ YES : MESH SIZE (mm)_____ ; % OF CONTEXT____   ☐ NO ☐ YES: VOLUME (L)_____ ; % OF CONTEXT

COINS (6.2.16)   INVENTORIED OBJECTS   PHOTOGRAPHS (5)

FINDS COLLECTED (6.2.17)

QUANTITY OF POTTERY COLLECTED_____ BASKET(S)_____ BOX(ES)

Deposit Sheet
Page 1

EXCAVATION NOTES (6.2.18)

Notes Continue?
☐ Yes   ☐ No

Deposit Sheet
Page 2

Corinth Excavations
American School of Classical Studies at Athens

Area_____

Context_____

Drawn by _____ Date _____ Scale ____ Top Plan Section Other Page __ of __

Drawing Sheet

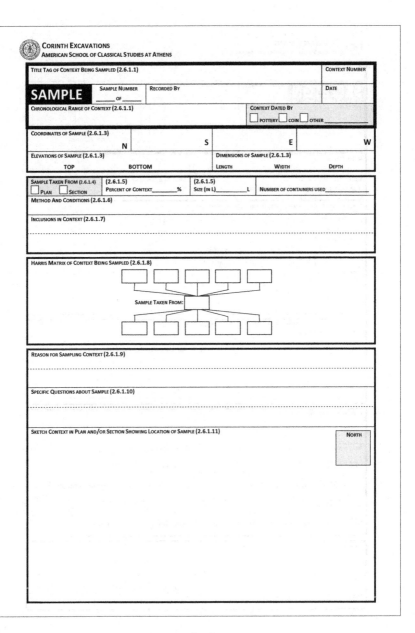

Sample Sheet

161

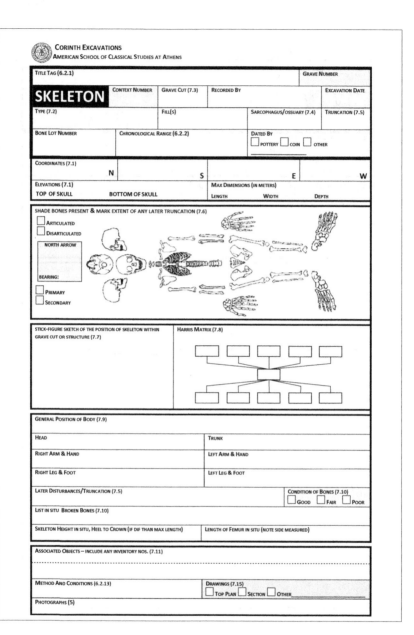

CORINTH EXCAVATIONS
AMERICAN SCHOOL OF CLASSICAL STUDIES AT ATHENS

TITLE TAG (6.2.1)					GRAVE NUMBER	

SKELETON	CONTEXT NUMBER	GRAVE CUT (7.3)	RECORDED BY		EXCAVATION DATE

TYPE (7.2)		FILL(S)		SARCOPHAGUS/OSSUARY (7.4)	TRUNCATION (7.5)

BONE LOT NUMBER | CHRONOLOGICAL RANGE (6.2.2) | DATED BY
☐ POTTERY ☐ COIN ☐ OTHER

COORDINATES (7.1)
N   S   E   W

ELEVATIONS (7.1)
TOP OF SKULL   BOTTOM OF SKULL

MAX DIMENSIONS (IN METERS)
LENGTH   WIDTH   DEPTH

SHADE BONES PRESENT & MARK EXTENT OF ANY LATER TRUNCATION (7.6)
☐ ARTICULATED
☐ DISARTICULATED
NORTH ARROW

BEARING:
☐ PRIMARY
☐ SECONDARY

STICK-FIGURE SKETCH OF THE POSITION OF SKELETON WITHIN GRAVE CUT OR STRUCTURE (7.7)

HARRIS MATRIX (7.8)

GENERAL POSITION OF BODY (7.9)

HEAD | TRUNK

RIGHT ARM & HAND | LEFT ARM & HAND

RIGHT LEG & FOOT | LEFT LEG & FOOT

LATER DISTURBANCES/TRUNCATION (7.5) | CONDITION OF BONES (7.10)
☐ GOOD ☐ FAIR ☐ POOR

LIST IN SITU BROKEN BONES (7.10)

SKELETON HEIGHT IN SITU, HEEL TO CROWN (IF DIF THAN MAX LENGTH) | LENGTH OF FEMUR IN SITU (NOTE SIDE MEASURED)

ASSOCIATED OBJECTS — INCLUDE ANY INVENTORY NOS. (7.11)

METHOD AND CONDITIONS (6.2.13) | DRAWINGS (7.15)
☐ TOP PLAN ☐ SECTION ☐ OTHER

PHOTOGRAPHS (5)

Skeleton Sheet
Page 1

EXCAVATION NOTES (7.14)

Notes Continue?
☐ YES ☐ NO

SPECIALIST OSTEOLOGICAL DATA (7.13)

GENERAL CONDITION OF BONES

BONES ABSENT (OR PRESENT, IF EASIER)

BONES BROKEN AND CAUSE(S) FOR BREAKAGE

ARTIFICIAL DEFORMATION (NOT INCLUDING GROUND PRESSURE)

OBSERVABLE PATHOLOGY

LENGTH, HEEL TO CROWN	LENGTH OF FEMUR

SIGNIFICANT MEASUREMENTS WHERE CONDITIONS ARE POOR

SEX	AGE					
☐ MALE ☐ FEMALE ☐ INDETERMINATE	☐ NEONATE ☐ INFANT ☐ CHILD ☐ ADOLESCENT ☐ ADULT ☐ INDETERMINATE

Skeleton Sheet
Page 2

TITLE TAG (6.4.1)

CONTEXT NUMBER

STRUCTURE

EXCAVATED?
☐ No ☐ YES

RECORDED BY

RECORDING DATE

LOT NUMBER

CHRONOLOGICAL RANGE (6.4.2)

DATED BY
☐ POTTERY ☐ COIN ☐ OTHER

COORDINATES (6.4.3)

N   S   E   W

ELEVATIONS (6.4.4)

TOP   BOTTOM

QUANTITY OF POTTERY COLLECTED _____ BASKET(S) _____ BOX(ES)

DIMENSIONS (6.4.5)

MATERIALS (6.4.6)

SIZE OF MATERIALS (6.4.7)

FINISH OF STONES (6.4.8)

MASONRY STYLE (6.4.9)

BONDING MATERIAL (6.4.10)

SPECIAL FEATURES (6.4.11)

HARRIS MATRIX (6.4.12)

RELATED CONTEXTS (6.4.15)

FORMATION/INTERPRETATION (6.4.13)

COLOR (6.2.6) – ONLY DESCRIBE SOIL IF STRUCTURE IS EXCAVATED

MODIFIER   HUE   COLOR   ☐ MIXED

INCLUSIONS (6.2.9)

COMPOSITION (6.2.7)

METHOD AND CONDITIONS (6.2.13)

DRAWINGS (4)
☐ TOP PLAN ☐ SECTION
OTHER _____

DRY SIEVING (6.4.16)
☐ No ☐ YES : MESH SIZE (mm) _____ ; % OF
CONTEXT _____

FLOTATION SAMPLES (6.2.15)
☐ No ☐ YES: VOLUME (L) _____ ; % OF
CONTEXT _____

COINS (6.4.17)

PHOTOGRAPHS (5)

FINDS COLLECTED (6.2.18)

Structure Sheet
Page 1

CORINTH EXCAVATIONS
AMERICAN SCHOOL OF CLASSICAL STUDIES AT ATHENS

NOTES (6.4.19)

Notes Continue?
☐ YES ☐ NO

Structure Sheet
Page 2

165

Working Harris Matrix Sheet

Made in the USA
Middletown, DE
06 February 2021